Rosl Schatzberger

Oma Goodness!

Austrian Magic in an English Kitchen

Illustrated by Yvonne Wise

Jessie's fund

MUSIC HELPING CHILDREN

Published in 2008

by Jessie's Fund
(Registered Charity no. 1045731)
15 Priory Street, York, YO1 6ET, UK
www.jessiesfund.org.uk

ISBN 978-0-9539121-1-7

Cover design by Clare Brayshaw

Prepared by:
York Publishing Services Ltd
64 Hallfield Road, Layerthorpe, York YO31 7ZQ
Tel: 01904 431213   Website: www.yps-publishing.co.uk

Printed in Great Britain

Rosl Schatzberger spent her childhood in Vienna before being forced to flee with her family in the weeks before the outbreak of the Second World War. The family settled in Manchester where, at a youth club for Austrian refugees, she met the Viennese boy who was to become her husband. Having had two children, she decided to utilise her love of cooking in forging a career, training as a Home Economist and then teaching in many different settings. Although she later re-trained as a social worker, and then as a family mediator, her passion for cooking remained central in her life and her desire to pass this on to her grandchildren, pictured with her here, was the starting point for this book. The one granddaughter to whom she cannot pass it on is Jessica, who died at the age of 9. This book is being sold in aid of the registered charity established in her memory.

Jessie's Fund helps seriously ill and disabled children to communicate by using music creatively and therapeutically. Most of the children we work with are not able to speak, and music can provide a vital means of expression. We give children in hospices all over the UK access to live music-making, providing instruments and training for care staff, and establishing posts for trained music therapists. Alongside our work with life-limited children we run creative projects in schools for children with special needs, and our support also extends to children in hospitals and other children's centres.

For more information about Jessie's Fund, please visit our website: www.jessiesfund.org.uk

Jessie's Fund, 15 Priory Street, York YO1 6ET, UK
Tel: 01904 658189. Email: info@jessiesfund.org.uk

Thanks to ...

Lesley, my daughter, for having confidence in my ability to produce this book and for her encouragement and clear guidance.

Wolfi (Marc), my husband, who has not only tasted all these recipes over many years, but has also given me unfailing help and advice along the way. He patiently made me come to terms with the computer, and without his help there would have been far more commas and capital letters! He has been my guide and support throughout my adult life, and it is his belief in me which has shaped my careers.

My grandchildren. To Jessica, without whom there would have been neither Fund nor book. To Hannah, Jacob, Tom, Katy, and Becca for their honest remarks (both positive and negative) about certain dishes, and for their suggestions of recipes to be included. Special thanks to Becca for her indexing input, and Jacob, who gave ideas about design.

My son Paul who, early in my culinary teaching career, took excellent photographs of dishes created at an exhibition by my students, thus giving impetus to, and encouragement for, my work.

My son-in-law Alan, whose proof-reading skills have been invaluable. The more professional eye of Anneliese Emmans Dean has been equally appreciated.

My friend Yvonne Wise, who readily agreed to create the beautiful, imaginative illustrations and, with her enthusiasm to carry out the task, spurred me on in a competitive way.

Lizzie Hoskin, for coming up with the title over the Friday evening chopped liver.

Victoria Wood, who became friends with Lesley at school, is Patron of Jessie's Fund, and was happy to contribute the Foreword.

Peter Gieler, for supporting me, and the Otto Harpner Fund of the Anglo-Austrian Society for financial assistance towards the publishing costs.

Last but not least, a big thank you to the rest of my family and the many friends with whom we have shared numerous meals, and whose appreciation and comments have inspired me and continue to do so.

Rosl Schatzberger
York, 2008

Contents

Foreword

OK, let's start with the positive stuff: I have written a foreword to a cookery book before, to Delia Smith's *Vegetarian Collection*. In which I had to confess I had never made anything of hers apart from the Christmas cake and the chocolate brownies.

Because really, I don't cook much. I can cook – I can read and I've got some pans, so it's not difficult. It's just that I don't really like it. Having had eating problems for most of my life, I still have an illogical feeling that a quarter of American hard gums and a bag of chips is quite a balanced and sophisticated meal.

Not that I'm blaming my parents – that book comes out next year – but unlike my school-mate Lesley's mother (author of this book), who was obviously happy to divvy up lovely nutritious interesting meals on a daily basis, my mother and father were a little bit kitchen shy. My mother had some culinary triumphs (I'm thinking of her corned beef hash and particularly her Spam curry), but once Clarence Birdseye worked out that a chicken pie could be frozen and sent to Bury, that was pretty much it in our house for ingredient assemblage.

Christmas dinner was the big exception. My father would do the whole thing, from running a frozen turkey under the hot tap to forgetting to top up the pudding steamer. We were never able to sit down to Christmas lunch before 4 o'clock in the afternoon, by which time we had eaten all of our selection boxes, watched *The Inn of the Sixth Happiness*, and we all hated each other.

But I will be very happy to have this book on my shelf, where no doubt it will lie, loved but untouched.

I am proud to be a supporter of Jessie's Fund. By buying this book, you're helping to enhance the lives of many children and their families. Thank you.

Victoria Wood

Introduction

There are many cookery books. This one is different. It mirrors one aspect of a satisfying and fulfilled life which has embraced wartime, emigration, a mixture of cultures, family and two careers.

'Oma, please can I have the recipe for … ?' That's how it started. How do you make Guglhupf, apple cake, Schnitzel, potato salad … ? The requests came by phone, email, letter or verbally during family meals.

When my son and daughter left home to go to university, I packed each of them off with a good kitchen knife, some basic pans and a small card index box with simple recipes. When grandchildren reached the same stage this was repeated, but their requests were a little more frequent and they demanded more elaborate dishes. I have always been happy to share recipes with family and friends, being careful not to omit that essential ingredient which makes a dish special or a method simpler. Aware of my ever-increasing interest, my friends would often give me unusual recipes, and sometimes old recipe books which they had inherited from their mothers or aunts.

Following the death of our little granddaughter Jessica in 1994, our family profile changed dramatically. The charity Jessie's Fund was founded by Jessica's parents (my daughter Lesley and her husband Alan), utilising the adrenalin caused by their grief. The primary goal of Jessie's Fund at that time was to embark on the task of introducing music therapy to all children's hospices in order to improve the quality of life for life-limited children. Fundraising is a constant challenge for any charity, and it was Lesley's proposal (motivated by the various vague suggestions I'd made over the years) that I should write a cookery book. Without hesitation I took up the challenge, imagining a modest little booklet with about 20 recipes. Lesley's ideas were slightly different, and so the project gathered momentum and grew, and grew. Part of this growth arose from the realisation that the mix of traditions to which the circumstances in my life had exposed me has made a huge impact on what I cook and how I do it.

I was born in Vienna, into a Jewish, assimilated family. I was, for my first 6 years, an only child in a family of childless aunts and uncles. The 1930s were years of depression and many women did not want to bring children into the world.

Although my mother's cooking influenced me greatly at a later stage, I was one of the few children in those days whose mother was working: she was running a small fashion shop in Vienna. My childless aunts were only too glad to take me on their shopping trips, and patiently let me help with the making of pasta, Strudels and dumplings.

I can still vividly remember the weekly walk to the Rochus Markt in Vienna, where fruit and vegetables were bountiful. I also recall my aunt smelling and feeling the fruit before eventually making a purchase. A magical event for me was watching a large red or white cabbage being put into what seemed like a huge machine which churned out vast quantities of finely shredded cabbage within seconds. This was long before the existence of food processors, and saved the cook a huge amount of time. These trips were enhanced by my getting either an ice cream in the summer or a hot sausage or baked potato in winter, which I tucked into on the way home.

My mother's food shopping was done differently. Her own shop was one of several in a busy street. There was a butcher, a baker, a grocer, a delicatessen and even a coffee-roasting shop. The memory still conjures up the totally distinctive aromas. My school day started at 8 o'clock in the morning and finished at 1 o'clock in the afternoon. On many occasions I went straight to my mother's shop, where I had lunch with her. She would give me a shopping list so that I could go and buy the ingredients for the meal of the day. Invariably I got little treats from the various shopkeepers: a couple of figs from the coffee shop (these were also roasted and used as an additive when brewing coffee), a strawberry cream-filled chocolate heart from the baker, a slice of salami from the butcher, and a pickled gherkin or a dollop of Sauerkraut from the grocer. I loved this job – it made me feel grown-up.

We, like most families, did not have an electric fridge, so shopping had to be done daily. But we did have a cold box, which looked rather like a blanket chest lined with metal. We had a regular supply of huge blocks of ice, delivered weekly and carried on the shoulder of the delivery men. We lived on the first floor of a four-storey apartment block, but these poor men had to deliver to customers on every floor. How things have changed!

After Hitler's entry into Austria in 1938, we had the good fortune to get a permit to come to England. Because of unemployment in England at the time, only those who were prepared to work as domestic servants were welcome. My parents were willing to do so, and we arrived in England (after spending a few months in Prague) in August 1939.

Watching my mother cooking unfamiliar recipes in a foreign kitchen, not understanding the language and yet creating amazing meals, was quite an education. My father acting as a butler brings to mind Fawlty Towers, and would have been amusing had it not been so heartbreaking.

Many of my recipes stem from those days, when food was rationed and money was scarce. But we ate well. I learnt to appreciate my mother's skill in making delicious, nourishing meals with very little money and modest ingredients, yet giving us the impression of abundance.

In England I joined an Austrian youth club, where I really continued my education. The club ran a very popular and successful restaurant in which I frequently served as a voluntary waitress. We collected money for the war effort, making thousands of chocolate truffles from powdered milk, cocoa and rum essence, which we sold at the restaurant. We even entertained workers in ammunition factories with our Austrian choir, conducted by my boyfriend and future husband, Wolfi. We went on several camping holidays, where my cooking skills were recognised, despite our having only the most basic equipment and ingredients. But I also experienced culinary disasters, the worst of which was when I made a trifle for Wolfi using salt instead of sugar. He still married me!

At a much later stage, by now a housewife with two children, I was able to extend my cooking skills, my favourite pastime being entertaining friends and family. I enrolled for a cookery course at a well-known Domestic Science college in Manchester. The first lesson was a revelation, and it pointed me to my future career.

After 3 years of enjoyable but hard work, I became a qualified Home Economist, and was fortunate to get the first job I applied for. It was in an adult education college, whose Principal was open to suggestions for running as many and as varied cookery classes as possible. So started a career which later included a wide range of teaching, from cordon bleu at one extreme to cookery therapy for people with mental health problems at the other. The work with people who had been institutionalised for most of their lives made me reassess my career, and I decided that I wanted to use my experience in an altogether different way.

This led me to social work, endorsed by Salford Social Services, who seconded me on a 3-year training course. Once qualified, I established a family centre in the most deprived area of that city, which provided a safe shelter for young parents who had failed at most things in their life. I tried, and sometimes succeeded, in giving them some confidence in their abilities. A successful Lancashire hotpot and apple pie sent a young mother home with a certain amount of pride.

From here I moved on to a very varied career in child care, at which point cooking became my relaxation therapy. Cooking and baking have brought me a great deal of pleasure for many years. When I stand at the cooker, stirring, mixing and even sometimes cursing, I feel as though I am putting something of myself into the food. Stirring with a special spoon bought on a holiday, cutting with an inherited knife, using an ancient spatula – they all conjure up memories.

Writing this book, I realise how food and cooking have shaped much of my life, and I have tried to ensure that readers know how and where recipes originated. My grandchildren often confuse unfamiliar recipes – yes, I still try out new ones – thinking they may be Austrian or Jewish, and sometimes they are neither.

Some of the recipes in this book may look strange and complicated on the printed page, but do have a try, and enjoy – go on!

Abbreviations

ml	millilitre	g	gram
tbs	tablespoon	kg	kilogram
dsp	dessert spoon	lb	pound
tsp	teaspoon	oz	ounce
(V)	suitable for vegetarians		

Equivalents

1000ml (1 litre)	1¾ pint	1lb	16oz	450g
575ml	1 pint	½lb	8oz	225g
275ml	½ pint	¼lb	4oz	110g
1 tbs	12ml	2oz	50g	
1 dsp	8ml			
1 tsp	5ml			

These equivalents are not exact. They are guidelines sufficiently accurate for cookery.

Temperatures

Celsius	Gas Mark	Fahrenheit	Description
110°	¼	225°	very cool
130°	½	250°	
140°	1	275°	cool
150°	2	300°	
170°	3	325°	moderate
180°	4	350°	
190°	5	375°	
200°	6	400°	moderately hot
220°	7	425°	hot
230°	8	450°	
240°	9	475°	very hot

If you have a fan oven, all temperatures should be reduced according to the manufacturer's instructions.

Quantities

Quantities in all recipes are sufficient for 4 people, unless otherwise stated.

Vorspeisen – Starters

Through the ages it has been usual for the sufficiently affluent to start a meal with a tasty small dish. Nowadays, food which was virtually unknown years ago is available in all the supermarkets. Holidays abroad, gap years spent travelling all over the world, cookery programmes on television – all these have changed our attitudes to food and increased our curiosity and desire to try new dishes.

I enjoy preparing these tasty morsels and believe that they can make an ordinary meal special. Most of the recipes I have chosen can be prepared in advance. They should not be too heavy; they are appetisers which should delight the eye as well as the stomach.

Unlike the French, Italian and now British cuisines, starters do not occupy a very important place in Austrian cookery, so this section tends to be more international than the rest of my book.

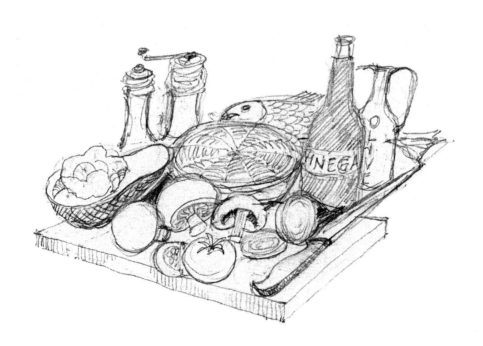

Avocado with Vinaigrette Dressing (V)

Avocados are a very versatile food, highly nutritious and, though almost unknown in northern Europe a couple of decades ago, they are readily available now. Even the simplest of dishes, such as avocado served with vinaigrette, makes a very pleasant start to a meal. Avocados are usually sold under-ripe, but they soon soften at room temperature, and when they feel slightly soft to the touch they are ready to be eaten. They will keep in the fridge for several days.

Ingredients

½ avocado per person
lemon juice

Vinaigrette

4 tbs wine vinegar
4 tbs olive oil
4 tbs water
1 clove of garlic, crushed
1 tsp sugar
½ tsp salt
a little black pepper
1 tsp Dijon mustard
chopped parsley or chives

Filling

chopped spring onion, chives, radishes, or a mixture of any of these, or else prawns with a light tomato-flavoured mayonnaise

Method

Halve avocados and remove stones.

Brush surface with lemon juice (stops discolouring).

Fill the hollow with any of the above filling ingredients.

Rapidly mix vinaigrette ingredients together, spoon over avocados.

Tip

Remove stones with a teaspoon. (I struggled for years with a small knife.)

Garnierte Eier – Egg Mayonnaise (V)

Ingredients

4 hard-boiled eggs
1 tbs mayonnaise
2 anchovies
½ tsp French mustard
1 tsp chopped capers
parsley
salt and pepper

Method

Halve eggs.

Carefully remove yolks from egg whites.

Sieve egg yolks (or mash).

Rinse and chop anchovies.

Mix egg yolks with mayonnaise, anchovies, capers and mustard, adding seasoning to taste.

Fill egg whites with this mixture.

Decorate with a caper and tiny parsley leaves.

Tip

Anchovies can be omitted for vegetarians.

French Egg and Tomato (V)

This French dish looks particularly appetising. We first got to know it when, many years ago, we treated ourselves to a meal in a 'posh' (i.e. expensive!) restaurant on the shores of Lake Annecy. Because we holidayed on limited budgets in those days, this was something of an occasion which unfortunately did not live up to our expectations. The main course was roast duck, the whole bird being served ceremoniously. A couple of mouthfuls were deposited on each plate, and that was the last we saw of our duck. But this particular hors d'oeuvre stood out and remained in our memories. Coincidentally, we had it again the following day in a much more modest setting – and it looked and tasted just as good.

Ingredients

    1 hard-boiled egg per person
    1 firm tomato per person
    vinaigrette (see Avocado, page 2) or mayonnaise
    chopped parsley or chives

Method

    Slice the tomatoes almost, but not quite, through. They will open out.

    Slice the eggs. (An egg slicer is helpful but not vital.)

    Slip a slice of egg into each cut of the tomato.

    Season, sprinkle with chopped herbs and a swirl of mayonnaise.

Russische Eier – Russian Eggs (V)

Well before the end of the Soviet era, we attended an international chamber music festival in Finland in which our daughter and son-in-law were taking part. At the end of this event we decided to take a 4-day excursion to what was then Leningrad (now St Petersburg). We enjoyed the beautifully maintained and exhibited museums and artefacts, did not enjoy the general drabness of place and people, and positively disliked the food provided. However, on our return to Helsinki we visited a Russian restaurant where we had one of the best meals we ever experienced. Here is a sample.

Ingredients

4 hard-boiled eggs
150g steamed mixed vegetables, cooled and diced
spring onions or ½ chopped onion
1 tsp chopped capers
1 tsp French mustard
mayonnaise to mix
salt and pepper

Method

Cut eggs in half lengthways, remove yolks and mash.

Mix yolks with vegetables, onions, capers, mustard, and mayonnaise.

Spoon or pipe into hollow egg whites.

Decorate with anchovy, a strip of tomato or chives (optional).

Serve on a bed of salad.

Tip

For speed you could use frozen mixed vegetables, brought to the boil and then cooled.

Gehackte Hühnerleber – Rough Liver Pâté
(Better known in my family as Chopped Liver)

This popular pâté is often served as a starter to a Friday night meal (Sabbath). At a time when chickens were a luxury food, only affordable for special occasions, every edible part of the bird was used. The whole chicken, along with the giblets, was used for soup. The skin of the neck was stuffed and roasted. The chicken, having provided the soup, was cut into portions, and with the addition of onions, chicken fat and crushed garlic, it was roasted until crisp and tasty. The liver was made into a pâté, any surplus fat was rendered down and used for cooking or as a spread for bread, and the crackling left from rendering was salted and eaten as a special treat with rye bread.

How differently we regard food these days. Chickens are relatively cheap, even if we choose organic or free-range ones, and most of us have neither the time, inclination or skills to cook in that manner. But those were the days before we knew about cholesterol, and when chicken fat was regarded as part of a wholesome diet. The following recipe has been adapted for the 21st century.

Ingredients
125g chicken liver (fresh, or available frozen in some large supermarkets)
2 hard-boiled eggs
½ onion
1 to 2 tbs corn oil
seasoning – pinch of salt and ground black pepper
pickled gherkin or olives (for garnish)

Method
Thoroughly defrost the liver if frozen.

Remove any parts with a bluish tinge (which would make it taste bitter).

Cover with water, add a little salt, and boil for 10 minutes.

Chop onion and hard-boiled eggs.

Chop cooked liver.

Add seasoning and enough oil to achieve a consistency suitable for spreading.

Garnish with pickled gherkin or olives.

Serve with crackers, toast or bread.

Tip

Although this can be made more speedily in a food processor, the result is bland and mushy, so it is worth putting in that little extra time to chop manually.

Eier mit Zwiebeln – Chopped Egg and Onion (V)
(We call this vegetarian Chopped Liver!)

Ingredients

2 hard-boiled eggs
½ onion
2 spring onions
1–2 tbs corn oil
seasoning – pinch of salt and ground black pepper
pickled gherkins or olives (for garnish)

Method

Chop onion, spring onions and hard-boiled eggs. Mix together.

Add seasoning and enough oil to achieve a consistency suitable for spreading.

Garnish with pickled gherkin or olives.

Serve with crackers, toast or bread.

Tip

For an extra sinful luxury, mix with butter instead of oil.

Gehackte marinierte Heringe – Chopped Herring

This is a well-known Jewish delicacy, emanating from Poland and Russia. Originally it was made from salt herrings, which is how herrings used to be preserved. I make it with rollmop herrings (sometimes known as pickled herrings), readily available either in glass jars or in plastic tubs at larger supermarkets. (There is a recipe for home-made rollmops later in this book – see page 38.)

Ingredients

2 pickled herrings and their vinegar
2 hard-boiled eggs, chopped
1 slice bread, preferably brown
2 ginger biscuits (optional)
1 small onion
1 small apple
1 tsp sugar
black pepper

Method

Remove herrings from container and soak bread and biscuits in the remaining vinegar for 5 minutes.

Drain bread through sieve and squeeze dry.

Using a food processor, intermittently whizz the herring until spreadable.

Chop all other ingredients.

Add bread and biscuits, onion, and apple to the herring, and mix together.

Add seasoning with enough sugar to achieve a piquant taste.

Add the chopped eggs.

Decorate by sprinkling on sieved hard-boiled egg yolk, or with sliced gherkins or olives.

Serve with matzo or cream crackers, or thin slices of rye bread.

Schwedische Heringe – Swedish Herring Salad

Ingredients

4 pickled herrings
2 eating apples, peeled
1 gherkin
½ onion
2 tbs mayonnaise
2 tbs yoghurt or sour cream
black pepper (salt may not be needed, as herrings are
   usually well seasoned)
1 tsp sugar (optional)

Method

Cut herrings into thin strips.

Chop onion and apples.

Slice gherkin.

Combine all ingredients, season to taste.

Serve with thinly sliced rye bread, or Pumpernickel (a very dark, dense, sour-ish bread), or crusty bread.

Waldorf Salad (V)

Some salads make interesting light hors d'oeuvres, and here is one of these. The name 'Waldorf' always triggers the memory of the episode of Fawlty Towers when an aggressive American guest demands, in the absence of any other available food, a 'simple Waldorf salad', and is gradually reduced to despair by Basil's combination of incompetence and rudeness. A hilarious scene – and below, a way to avoid it!

Ingredients

4 eating apples
3 sticks celery
100g chopped walnuts
1 tsp lemon juice
1 tbs mayonnaise with 1 tbs yoghurt
salt and pepper
a little sugar

Method

Peel and chop apples. Chop celery.
Mix mayonnaise, yoghurt and lemon juice.
Combine all ingredients. Season to taste.
Serve on a plate of salad leaves.

Tip

This dish looks spectacular when using large red apples. Hollowed out and carefully leaving the outside intact, they can be stuffed with the salad. They make a good starter for Christmas dinner, too. Provided the apples are brushed with lemon juice, they can be prepared a few hours in advance.

Grapefruit – Grilled or Baked (V)

Although normally regarded as a breakfast food, grapefruit served this way really makes a very pleasant starter.

Ingredients

½ grapefruit per person
knob of butter
1 tsp demerara (brown) sugar
sprinkling of cinnamon or ginger
1 dsp rum or brandy (optional, but recommended)

Method

Pre-heat oven to 170°C / gas mark 3, or pre-heat grill.

Cut grapefruit in half.

Loosen segments.

Melt butter and brush on open grapefruit halves.

Sprinkle with sugar.

Add a dash of rum or brandy.

Either bake for 25 minutes or grill until bubbly.

Mushrooms with Greek Yoghurt (V)

Ingredients

200g button mushrooms
100ml Greek yoghurt or sour cream
4 tbs tomato ketchup
¼ tsp Worcester sauce
1 clove garlic, crushed
2 tbs mayonnaise

Method

Slice mushrooms, or just halve them if they are small.

Mix all other ingredients.

Add mushrooms.

Adjust seasoning to taste. A little lemon juice may be needed.

Serve surrounded by watercress or rocket.

Liptauer Dip

Dips are a wonderful food to share, be it at a party, pre-dinner or a picnic. They can be served with pitta bread, cheese biscuits, crisps, matzo crackers, or raw vegetables (crudités). I was introduced to them in the USA many years ago and enjoyed the informality which they seemed to encourage. They have since become very popular over here and are available ready made, but they are fun to make yourself and you can use ingredients of your choice.

In Austria, Liptauer is often used as a sandwich filling. During times of scarcity it was a way of making a little cheese go a long way. It is a good opportunity to use small bits of left-over cheese, which I grate and refrigerate for this purpose.

Ingredients

100g cheese (opinions vary as to whether strong or mild),
or cream cheese
50g butter or margarine
½ small onion, finely chopped
1 tsp chopped capers (good, but optional)
2 chopped anchovies (or ½ tsp anchovy paste)
1 tsp French mustard
½ tsp caraway seeds
1 level tsp sweet paprika (not the fiery type!)
pepper and salt if necessary (depending on cheese)

Method

Grate cheese as finely as possible.

Mix all ingredients.

To serve, sprinkle with a little extra paprika and chopped chives.

Israeli Carrot Dip (V)

You can spend a whole evening having dips of various kinds and chatting, or you can have them with an apéritif before starting a meal, and of course you can use selected dips, suitably presented, as a starter. Such versatility has led to dips made of all sorts of ingredients being invented by us enthusiasts. Here is one which I believe originated in Israel.

Ingredients

500g carrots
½ onion
1 clove garlic, crushed
2 tbs olive oil
juice of 1 lemon
1/3 tsp ground cumin
parsley
pepper and salt

Method

Peel and cook carrots until only just soft ('al dente').

Put all ingredients into liquidiser, or chop and mash with fork.

Season for piquancy to taste.

Mackerel Pâté

The humble mackerel can be very tasty, especially when smoked.

Ingredients

150g smoked mackerel
75g cream cheese or Greek yoghurt
1 small clove garlic, crushed
a few drops lemon juice
pepper
pinch of cayenne pepper (optional)
thinly sliced cucumber, tomatoes or peppers for decoration

Method

Skin fish and mash.

Add all other ingredients, except decoration.

Decorate with cucumber, tomatoes or peppers.

Serve with curls of lemon and crackers, crispbreads or Melba toast.

This recipe can also be made with smoked salmon (cheaply available trimmings are fine) or kippers.

Tip

To make Melba toast, toast thick slices of white bread. With a sharp knife, cut in half horizontally, then cut into triangles. Put on a baking tray, bake in oven at 180°C / gas mark 4 until curled and crisp.

Suppen — Soups

Soups are an essential part of the Austrian menu. No meal is complete without a plate of steaming soup, almost regardless of the weather.

There are three basic types of soup:

1   Clear soups with a garnish. The soup then often acquires the name of the garnish used. It is based on good chicken or beef stock.

2   Puréed soups.

3   Vegetable soups, with chunky bits of vegetables, thickened with a roux.

All of these are greatly improved by using a good stock, either meat based or vegetable based. If time is short, stock cubes are very helpful, but if used too often there is a danger of all soups having a similar taste. It is also worth remembering that their salt content is rather high, so only use them when necessary.

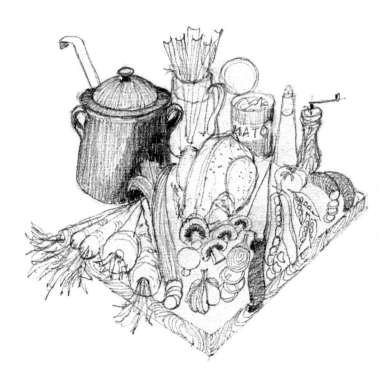

Hühnersuppe (or Hendelsuppe) – Chicken Soup

There are a lot of myths about 'Mama's Jewish Chicken Soup'. I doubt its nutritional value or its curative properties, but I can vouch for its popularity. It is certainly light, tasty, and a firm favourite with all the family. A pinch of saffron is occasionally added to enhance the colour. I remember my mother telling me that when she was a child her own mother used to send her out to buy a 'thimbleful' of saffron for the chicken soup.

For the original recipe you require a whole boiling chicken, not a young roasting bird. Old hens have a stronger flavour, but are not readily available. The following recipe is therefore adapted to modern times and easily available ingredients.

Ingredients

1 medium-sized chicken (or about 1kg chicken wings or legs)
1 onion, washed, not peeled (the skin provides colour)
1 clove garlic
1 carrot
a few celery sticks, including leaves
parsley, including stalks
1 small parsnip
1 tsp salt
6 black peppercorns
water to cover the chicken

Method

Rinse the inside of the chicken.

Put into a large pan, add the coarsely cut-up vegetables and the seasoning.

Cover with cold water. Slowly bring to boil.

Skim grey sediments gathering on top.

Simmer gently for approximately 2 hours.

When cool, strain through a sieve. It is optional whether you include some of the vegetables (sliced) or not. I always add a few slices of carrot for colour, and squeeze the rest to extract the flavour.

In my mother's day, before cholesterol was counted and before central heating, people needed all the calories they could get, and the fatter the soup, the more nourishing it was deemed to be. However, now we refrigerate the soup overnight and remove the congealed fat from the top. Heat, taste, adjust seasoning, and add any of the following garnishes: vermicelli, any other small pasta previously boiled (al dente), semolina or matzo dumplings (see next recipe), or even beaten egg and mashed sweetcorn.

The boiled chicken meat can be used for stir-fry, chicken and mushroom pies, and curry.

Soup Garnishes

Semolina or Matzo Dumplings (V)

Ingredients

75g soft margarine
100g matzo meal or semolina
1 egg
salt and pepper

Method

Mix above ingredients with wet hands, shape into 2cm balls and drop into boiling soup.

Boil gently until they rise to the top.

Fridatten – Pancake Strips (V)

An excellent use for left-over pancakes. Fridattensuppe often appears as the staple soup in the set meals of the day served in Austrian Gasthäuser (pubs) or even hotels and restaurants.

Method

Cut pancakes into narrow strips.

Add to boiling soup just before serving.

Chinese-style Egg (V)

Ingredients

1 egg (1 egg white will do)
1 tsp cornflour
3–4 tbs sweetcorn (puréed)
salt and pepper

Method

Mix and whisk into boiling soup.

Boil for 2–3 minutes.

Serve.

Austrian-style Egg (V)

Ingredients

1 egg

Method

Add beaten egg to soup.

Whisk until it coagulates.

Serve with chopped parsley.

Rindsuppe – Austrian Beef Broth

This is a famous Viennese speciality, served in the best restaurants as well as in simple Beisln (pubs/bistros), often followed by Tafelspitz (beef that has been boiled in the broth) with creamed spinach. It is worth noting that the word 'Menü' has a different meaning in Austria. It means the set meal of the day, rather than a list of available dishes. To get a menu listing available dishes, you ask for 'die Speisekarte'.

Ingredients

> 1kg silverside of beef (or a more economical piece of lean brisket)
> beef bones (if available)
> 1 onion
> 1 carrot
> 1 celery stick
> 1 clove of garlic
> 1 bouquet garni
> salt and pepper or peppercorns
> parsley
> 1 litre water

Method

> Wash meat and bones. Roughly chop vegetables.
>
> Put meat, bones and vegetables into pan, then cover with cold water.
>
> Add seasoning.
>
> Slowly bring to boil, then simmer for approximately 2 hours until meat is tender. (Time needed depends on cut of beef.)
>
> Leave meat in liquid until cool. (This makes it moister.)
>
> Skim fat off top and strain soup.
>
> Serve the clear soup with any of the garnishes mentioned for Chicken Soup (page 20), sprinkled with chopped parsley or chives.
>
> The remaining meat is thickly sliced, and usually served with garlic-flavoured creamed spinach, or any other vegetable, and potatoes.

Zwiebelsuppe – French Onion Soup (V)

At its best when made by my husband; at its worst when accidentally landing on his lap in a restaurant, when he was all dressed up to visit the Royal Opera House. The smell, so deliciously appetising normally, was an embarrassment in the theatre and did not enhance our enjoyment of the performance.

Ingredients

500g onions
25g butter and 1 dsp oil
1 tsp salt
¼ tsp sugar
1 litre stock
black pepper
1 tbs brandy, just before serving (optional)

Garnish

1 round of French bread per person
Strong cheese (Gruyère or Cheddar)

Method

Melt fat, then fry onions, adding sugar.

Fry slowly until a rich brown colour is achieved. (Sugar helps it to caramelise.)

Add stock. Simmer for 1 hour.

Add salt and freshly ground black pepper.

Adjust seasoning to taste.

To serve: toast bread, top with cheese, put under grill until melted, and float on each bowl of soup.

Erbsensuppe – Fresh Pea Soup (V)

This firm favourite with all my family seems to capture the essence of spring when made with fresh peas and parsley, although it can also be made with frozen peas.

I have wonderful childhood memories of sitting in the sunny garden of a holiday cottage in Austria, shelling peas. My mother always had to buy a double quantity of peas because it was understood that for every pea going into the pot there was one for my mouth.

When giving this soup to my granddaughters many years ago, the roux was not as smooth as it should have been and Jessica remarked: 'Oma, I love these dumplings.' It just shows what grandmothers can get away with!

Ingredients

500g peas in their pods, shelled
25g butter – if you want that special taste, it has to be butter
1 tbs flour
1 litre stock
1 tbs chopped parsley
salt and pepper
25g vermicelli

Method

Put shelled peas into the stock and bring to boil, adding a few pods (to be removed later).

Boil until tender.

Make a roux, i.e. melt butter in a pan, add flour, cook until nut brown.

Add stock gradually. Stir well to get rid of any lumps.

Add remaining stock (with peas) and bring to boil.

Add vermicelli and simmer until they are 'al dente'.

Add chopped parsley.

Gulaschsuppe – Goulash Soup

A popular soup in Vienna, often served in the early hours of Sylvester (New Year), but available all year round at the various Gasthofs and restaurants.

Skiing holidays in Austria are memorable for many things, not least for their goulash soups served in the wooden chalets/restaurants on the mountain peaks or at the tops of the pistes.

Ingredients

250g stewing steak (shin or skirt)
2 Frankfurters (smoked sausages – optional)
250g potatoes, cubed
2 medium onions, chopped
1 dsp oil
½ tsp paprika
1 tbs tomato purée
1 tbs flour
½ tsp caraway seeds
marjoram (optional)
1 litre stock or water
pepper and salt to season
½ tsp vinegar

Method

Heat oil in pan, and add onion. Fry until onions are a rich brown colour.

Add meat, sliced into thin strips. Increase heat, and fry quickly.

Add potatoes, spices and seasoning.

Add flour, stirring well until all ingredients are coated.

Add stock and stir.

Simmer until meat is tender.

Add thinly sliced Frankfurters, if used.

Season to taste. Add a dash of vinegar.

Serbische Bohnensuppe — Serbian Bean Soup

We first tasted this soup whilst on a holiday in what was then Yugoslavia. We spent a day at a beach and had lunch under somewhat unusual circumstances: not everybody was attired! Everybody, of all shapes, ages and sizes, had lunch at long tables and benches in the shade of a large wooden building, euphemistically calling itself a restaurant. The dress code was 'come as you are'. The only dish on offer was Serbian Bean Soup. For my husband, soup has never tasted as good since. But even if eaten under more conventional circumstances, it is a very tasty soup, which can easily be transformed into a more substantial dish by increasing the quantity of sausage, and adding cubes of potatoes.

Ingredients

100g dried haricot or butter beans, soaked overnight,
    or 1 medium tin of either
50g chopped smoked sausage, bacon or Frankfurters
1 onion, chopped
1 clove garlic, crushed
1 medium potato cut into 1cm cubes
1 tbs olive oil or butter
1 level tbs flour
1 tbs tomato purée
1 level tsp sweet paprika
a pinch of dried marjoram
1 bay leaf
1 litre stock or water and liquid from tinned beans and
    Frankfurters, if used
seasoning to taste

Method

Heat oil, fry bacon and add onion.

Add flour. Cook until a rich brown colour.

Gradually add hot stock, stirring in a figure of 8 to get rid of lumps.

Add paprika, tomato purée, spices and seasoning. Stir well.

Add potatoes, beans, and sliced sausage and cook until tender.

Add seasoning to taste.

Kartoffel (und Schwammerl) Suppe – Potato (and Mushroom) Soup (V)

It is easy to make this tasty soup using staple items from the vegetable rack. Delicious with just potatoes and onions, it can be varied by the addition of mushrooms, and even by using butterbeans instead of potatoes. Note that in Austria the word 'Erdäpfel' is sometimes used for potatoes instead of 'Kartoffeln'.

Ingredients

1 medium onion, chopped
1 or 2 potatoes, diced
100g mushrooms, sliced
50g butter or oil
50g plain flour
1 litre stock or water
salt and pepper to taste
½ tsp caraway seeds (optional, but adding to authenticity)
parsley or chives (for garnish)

Method

Melt butter or oil.

Add potatoes, mushrooms, onions. Fry for 5 minutes.

Add flour, stir well, and cook until golden brown.

Add stock, seasoning, and seeds.

Simmer for approximately 30 minutes.

Adjust seasoning to taste.

Serve sprinkled with chopped parsley or chives.

_____

Tip

_____

For non-vegetarians, this soup can be bulked up with slices of sausage, turning it into a satisfying meal.

Linsensuppe – Green Lentil Soup (V)

A nourishing and warming soup, using store cupboard ingredients. The meat element can be omitted for a vegetarian soup.

Ingredients

125g green lentils
1 large onion
1 carrot, sliced
1 stick celery, sliced
1 tbs flour
1 tbs butter (or oil)
1 litre water or stock
seasoning
a small handful of vermicelli
either a ham bone, or 2 rashers of chopped, smoked bacon
    (optional)

Method

Wash and strain lentils.

Chop onion and fry until golden (with bacon, if used).

Add other vegetables. Fry for 5 minutes.

Add flour. Stir until absorbed.

Add lentils, water or stock, ham bone if used, and seasoning.

Simmer for approximately 30 minutes or until lentils are tender.

Remove ham bone if used.

Add vermicelli, and cook for a further few minutes.

Adjust seasoning to taste.

Karfiolsuppe – Cauliflower Soup (V)

Ingredients

- 1 small or half a large cauliflower (broccoli can be used as an alternative)
- 1 litre water or stock
- ¼ litre milk
- salt and pepper
- 1 handful of chopped parsley
- 1 tbs flour
- 1 tbs butter (there is no substitute for the authentic taste), or oil if you must

Method

Cut cauliflower into small florets, including some green leaves.

Simmer gently until barely soft.

Make roux with butter or oil and flour.

Cook roux until it goes a russet colour, add boiling stock gradually, beating out all lumps.

Add cauliflower to soup. Season to taste.

Add chopped parsley or chives just before serving.

Tip

If a smoother soup is preferred, remove a few florets for garnish, and purée the rest.

Paradeissuppe – Tomato Soup (V)

In competition with Heinz Tomato Soup (which, according to my husband and youngest grandson, I have not won) I will nevertheless give my own version, which I believe to be healthier and certainly more economical when made in quantities suitable for a family. Incidentally, I believe the word 'Paradeiser' for 'Tomaten' is not used in German-speaking countries other than Austria, and is possibly known only in Vienna.

Ingredients

1 medium tin (400g) of tomatoes
1 tbs flour
25g butter or olive oil
1 tbs tomato purée
½ litre stock
juice of ½ lemon
1 tsp sugar
salt and pepper
snipped basil or chopped parsley (for garnish)
1 tbs boiled rice (optional)

Method

Melt butter or oil, add flour, and cook until nut brown.

Add hot stock gradually to make a roux.

Add tomatoes, tomato purée, liquid and seasoning. Purée with blender or otherwise.

Add rice, if using.

Taste, adjust seasoning, add garnish.

Optional: add 1 tsp cream to float on top of each dish or, for a healthier version, a small tin of evaporated milk whisked into the soup before serving.

Gemüsesuppe – Spring Vegetable Soup (V)

I make this soup on the day I have bought the weekly fresh vegetables and I can pinch a little bit of everything – there is virtually no cost involved. Or at the end of the week, I use what is left in the vegetable rack.

Ingredients

portion of cauliflower separated into florets
1 carrot, sliced
1 stick celery, sliced
1 onion, chopped
1 leek, chopped
1 potato, cubed
2 tomatoes, skinned
2 tbs peas (fresh or frozen)
any other available vegetables
50g plain flour
50g butter (oil can be substituted)
1 litre stock
salt and pepper
chopped parsley or chives

Method

Put vegetables and stock into pan. Bring to the boil.

Add seasoning and simmer until barely tender.

Make a roux by melting butter in a separate pan, adding flour, and cooking until russet brown. Then add a few ladles of the hot vegetable liquid gradually, stirring vigorously to break down lumps.

Add this mixture to the soup and bring to boil.

Serve sprinkled with parsley or chives.

Gerstlsuppe — Winter Broth

One of the most welcoming of soups on a damp, cold day.

Ingredients

    a meat bone (ham shank is ideal)
    2 carrots
    2 sticks celery, including green leaves
    1 onion
    200g broth mix readily available in supermarkets, or:
        50g barley
        75g green split lentils
        75g red split lentils
    4 tbs butterbeans (or other dried white beans)
    1½ litres of stock
    salt and pepper

Method

    Cover cereals, pulses and beans with plenty of water and soak overnight.

    Drain and rinse.

    Chop vegetables finely.

    Put all ingredients into large pan, cover with liquid.

    Add bone and seasoning.

    Cover and simmer for approximately 2 hours.

    When the soup is ready, the lentils will have turned into a purée.

    Remove bone, taste soup, and adjust seasoning as required.

Corn Chowder (V)

The first time I was served this soup was in a restaurant in San Francisco. It was in the middle of summer and I was dressed accordingly. To my shock and surprise, it was blowing a gale – not unusual I was told. A plate of soup was therefore very inviting. The combination of sweetcorn with vegetables was excellent. I have been making it ever since.

Ingredients

25g butter or oil
1 tbs flour
1 onion, chopped
1 green pepper, diced
100g mushrooms, sliced
1 litre stock
1 medium tin (400g) of sweetcorn, puréed
2 medium potatoes, diced
salt and pepper
small carton single cream (optional)
chopped parsley or chives

Method

Fry onion in butter until golden.

Add flour. Stir until lightly coloured.

Add hot liquid gradually, stirring to get rid of any lumps.

Add cut up vegetables and sweetcorn. Simmer until tender.

The chowder can be puréed, but I prefer it chunky.

Season to taste, add cream and chopped herbs.

Courgette and Tomato Soup (V)

This is a very useful recipe when courgettes are in season, or when they turn to marrows. It contains no flour, depends for its consistency on puréed vegetables, is delicious, and on top of all this, it is also healthy and ideal for slimmers.

Ingredients

500g courgettes (or marrow)
1 medium tin tomatoes
1 medium onion
1 clove garlic (optional)
salt and pepper to taste
chopped parsley or chives (for garnish)

Method

Chop onion, and fry in a lightly greased pan.

Add crushed garlic.

Roughly cut courgettes and tomatoes. Add seasoning.

Simmer until tender.

Purée with blender.

Adjust seasoning, and if necessary add water or stock to achieve the desired consistency.

Serve with garnish of chopped parsley or chives.

Fisch – Fish

My childhood memories of fish in meals are very limited. Being totally land-locked, Austria has never had the abundance of fish we know in Britain, and my experience was primarily of fish – any fish – which was egg-and-bread-crumbed and fried. Trout, which used to be caught in the many Austrian streams and rivers, were highly priced. Restaurants frequently keep fish alive in tanks and you order and pay for them by weight. You cannot get them fresher, and they taste superb. Alas, trout farms are beginning to appear.

The following recipes are a collection, mostly from friends and relatives, which I have gathered during my travels. Jewish cooks have always made excellent use of cheap fish such as herring, abundantly available in Poland and Russia, which they usually pickled and/or salted to preserve them (before the age of freezers).

With the current emphasis on healthy nutrition, herrings are recommended for their rich source of Omega 3, so the recipes included here may be of increased interest. The small but sometimes irritating little bones in herrings will dissolve in the vinegary solution if left for 1 or 2 days. Pickled herrings will keep in the fridge for up to 3 days.

Soused Herrings

Ingredients

4 herrings, scaled and filleted
1 medium onion, thinly sliced
100ml wine vinegar, mixed with 75ml water
1 level tbs honey or syrup
1 dsp sugar

Seasoning

1 bay leaf
6 peppercorns
salt and pepper

Method

Pre-heat oven to 150°C / gas mark 2.

Season herrings, sprinkle with onion, and roll up from tail.

Pack tightly into a shallow, ovenproof dish.

Cover with sliced onions, vinegar mixture, and seasoning. The liquid should reach the top of the fish.

Sprinkle with sugar, and drizzle honey over the top.

Cover loosely with foil.

Bake for approximately 1 hour, or until the herrings are a rich brown, and the liquid reduced by half.

Bratheringe – Marinaded Herrings

Ingredients

4 herrings, scaled and filleted
salt and pepper
flour to coat herring
oil for frying
1 onion, thinly sliced

Vinaigrette

2 tbs corn oil (olive oil has too distinctive a flavour)
3 tbs white wine vinegar
½ chopped onion
1 tsp capers, chopped
1 tsp sugar
seasoning

Method

Season herrings, then coat with flour.

Fry in shallow oil until brown on both sides.

Place into a shallow casserole, and cover with thin slices of onion.

Mix vinaigrette ingredients together and cover herrings with vinaigrette.

Leave for at least 24 hours in fridge to marinade.

Rollmops — Pickled Herrings

My husband tells me that, when he was a young boy in Vienna, pickled herrings were sold at corner grocers' shops out of big, wooden barrels. He was passionately fond of the onions which usually went with the herrings, and when his mother occasionally sent him to buy some herrings, and he tried to persuade the grocer to give him more than his fair share of onions, the grocer was unco-operative. It still rankles with him more than 70 years later!

Back to the present. It is useful to make lots of this at one time as it will keep in the fridge for several days and will also freeze well.

Ingredients

  5 large herrings, filleted
  2 tbs cooking salt
  2 large onions, sliced into thin rings
  2 cups distilled vinegar
  ½ cup water
  4 tbs sugar
  1 dsp pickling spice
  1 bay leaf

Method

  Cover herrings with salt and leave overnight.

  Rinse and pat dry.

  Put herrings in layers, with the thinly sliced onion rings, in a suitable dish.

  Heat remaining ingredients gently until sugar is dissolved.

  Cover herrings with vinegar mixture when cooled slightly.

  Allow to marinade for 24 hours before eating.

Garnished with pickled cucumber, hard-boiled eggs and olives, this makes a very good starter. If accompanied by a potato salad or any other salad of your choice, it makes a tasty main course.

Salmon

Years ago salmon was a luxury food, only served for special occasions, and usually lavishly decorated, sometimes on a bed of gelée. Because of its size it was, and still is, a wonderful food for entertaining. Nowadays, however, salmon is mostly farmed, plentiful and relatively cheap. Sadly, this is at the expense of flavour and texture. If you can get a freshly caught wild salmon, treat it with respect, but even the farmed variety can be made into some excellent meals, both hot and cold.

To Boil a Whole Salmon

Ask the fishmonger to scale the fish and to trim it, though you may want to leave the head on for the purpose of presentation.

Although the method of cooking salmon is simple, it is very easy to overcook it. So, here are my tips to avoid this:

- Put the salmon into a large pan (or fish kettle), and cover with cold water.
- Add 4 tsp salt and a few grinds of pepper.
- Cover the pan, and bring slowly to the boil. (This should take about 30 minutes.)
- Allow it to simmer gently for 8 minutes, then turn off the heat and allow the fish to cool in the liquid.
- Skin the fish before serving.

To Bake a Whole Salmon

This is by far the easiest method, since not many of us have a fish kettle or sufficiently large casserole.

Pre-heat the oven to 180°C / gas mark 4.

Season the salmon well.

Wrap loosely in a large, well-oiled sheet of foil.

Bake for 1 hour.

Leave for 15 minutes before unwrapping. The skin will peel off very easily.

Many recipes give all sorts of ingredients to add, such as wine, lemon juice, herbs etc., but I believe the flavour and the colour of the fish are best if it is cooked in its natural juice.

Salmon Steaks can be baked in the same manner as the whole fish, taking about 20 minutes.

Mackerel in Egg and Lemon Sauce

Mackerel are a very rich source of Vitamin A and D, but be warned: only buy them when really fresh. On a caravan holiday in Cornwall, we were able to buy freshly caught mackerel from local fishermen just returning with their catch. They were almost giving them away. We cooked them on our camping stove and, although it was decades ago, I still remember this delicious meal. The following recipe is a little more elaborate.

Ingredients

    2 mackerel, filleted and cut into 4 portions
    1 onion, thinly sliced
    3 tbs sugar
    1 tsp salt
    ground pepper
    water to barely cover the fish

Sauce

    2 eggs
    juice of 2 lemons
    1 cup of fish stock
    1 level tsp cornflour

Method

    In a wide saucepan bring water, onion, seasoning, and sugar to boil.

    Add the fish. Partially cover, and simmer gently for about 20 minutes.

    Place fish fillets into a serving dish.

    Boil liquid to reduce it to 1 cupful.

    Beat eggs. Add fish liquid and lemon juice.

    Add cornflour mixed with a little cold water.

    Put into a small saucepan and cook until mixture coats the spoon. Stir constantly, and do not allow to boil.

    Taste and adjust seasoning.

    Pour sauce over mackerel, and garnish with lemon slices.

See overleaf for tip

Tip

This method can also be used to cook fillets of halibut for a special occasion.

Gefillte Fish – Jewish-style Chopped Fish

This is very popular food in Jewish households. It originated in Eastern Europe, with fish from the Baltic Sea and fresh-water lakes. Fish from these sources are primarily bream, carp and pike, in contrast to the haddock, cod and hake (all sea fish) most commonly eaten in Britain.

My grandmother, who originated from Poland, would buy a whole carp and stuff it with a mixture of chopped carp and other fish. Families were large in those days, and the quantities of fish used were correspondingly large. One reason for chopping the fish and using it as a sort of forcemeat was to make it easier and safer for children to eat: these freshwater fish are rather bony, and in filleting and chopping them, the bones can be removed.

Nowadays a mixture of fish is shaped into patties, and either poached in stock, cooked in a sweet-and-sour tomato sauce, or fried. The fish used tends to be a mixture of haddock, cod, hake, and whiting. Because it is quite a laborious job, and because these dishes will keep in the fridge for about 2 days and also freeze well, it is worth using at least 1kg of fish. Although a mixture of fish is ideal, I have on occasions just used one type of fish, with reasonable results. It is a matter of personal choice, cost and availability.

Basic Gefillte Fish Mixture

Ingredients *(Makes about 12–15 patties)*
    500g haddock
    500g cod
    1 medium onion, chopped
    2 tbs oil
    2 tsp sugar
    2 tsp salt
    2 eggs
    4 tbs medium matzo meal (or breadcrumbs made from
       matzo crackers or toast)
    freshly ground black pepper

Method

Skin and bone the fish (or ask the fishmonger to do this). If intending to poach the fish (see page 46), keep the trimmings for stock.

Either chop the fish with a sharp knife, or use the food processor (in short bursts only).

If using a processor, add onion, eggs and oil, processing until blended. Then add remaining ingredients and mix lightly.

If doing it by hand, add all other ingredients to chopped fish and mix well.

The mixture should be firm enough to hold its shape; it may be necessary to add a little water if too stiff, or more matzo meal if too soft.

With wet hands, shape into patties.

This is the basic mixture to be used in the following three recipes.

Chopped Fried Fish

Ingredients

1 quantity of basic Gefillte Fish mixture

a good supply of either dry fine breadcrumbs (not the coloured variety), or

medium matzo meal, or

finely crushed cornflakes

vegetable oil for frying

Method

Put the coating crumbs on a sheet of paper and roll the patties into them until well coated.

Pour about 2cm depth of oil into a frying pan and heat. The oil should be really hot.

Leaving enough room in the pan to turn the patties, fry them for about 3 minutes on each side, until deep brown.

Drain on paper.

Enjoy the distinctive aroma (or get the extractor fan blowing!)

Boiled Gefillte Fish – Poached Fish Patties

Ingredients

1 quantity of basic Gefillte Fish mixture

Stock

bones and skin of fish (or fish stock cube)
   in approximately ¼ litre water
1 medium onion, chopped
1 carrot, sliced
1 level tsp sugar
salt and pepper

Method

Bring stock, sugar, seasoning, and fish trimmings to boil. Simmer for 15 minutes.

Remove bones and skin.

Make patties from the fish mixture, as on page 44.

Carefully add them to the stock with onion and carrot. The liquid should cover the fish – add water if necessary.

Bring to boil and reduce the heat to a bare simmer for about 45 minutes.

Lift the patties out of the stock with a slotted spoon and put them into a deep serving dish.

Decorate each one with a slice of carrot from the stock. Pour over the reduced fish stock. Leave to cool.

This dish is usually eaten cold, and served with beetroot and horseradish pickle.

Chopped Fish in a Piquant Sauce

Ingredients

1 quantity of basic Gefillte Fish mixture

Sauce

1 tin of chopped tomatoes or passata
1 onion
1 green pepper, chopped
1 tsp sugar
salt and pepper to taste
fresh basil (for garnish)

Method

Pre-heat the oven to 150°C / gas mark 2.

Fry onion until golden.

Add green pepper, tomatoes, sugar, and seasoning.

Simmer until mixture is thick. Put into ovenproof casserole.

Make patties from the fish mixture, as on page 44.

Add patties to sauce and cover.

Bake for about 50 minutes, basting once or twice.

Garnish with a sprinkling of fresh basil and serve with pasta, rice or potatoes.

Sulz Fisch – Poached Salmon in Gelée

This recipe also originated in Eastern Europe, and was handed down to me by my mother. Originally it was always made with carp, and I well remember buying a whole fish, and watching my mother or the fishmonger clean it and chop it into portions. Most of all, I can remember a large sac which, I was told, was its bladder. I am not sure of the correctness of this biological information. I have adapted this recipe and initially used eel when available; also, occasionally, mackerel, but I find that salmon gives by far the best result. It is unusual, but ethnic and very tasty.

Ingredients

1kg salmon cut into steaks (or fillets will do)
700g onion, coarsely chopped
1 dsp sugar
1 tsp salt
6 peppercorns
skin, bones and head of salmon, if available (ask your fishmonger)
thinly pared rind and juice of ½ lemon
50g finely chopped walnuts (optional)

Method

Put onion and spices into large, shallow pan (I use a large frying pan).

Add 150ml water, bones, skin etc. (This will help the liquid to gel when cold.)

Cover and simmer for 10 minutes.

Remove skin and bones.

Add fish steaks (the liquid should just cover the fish).

Simmer gently for 20 minutes.

Arrange fish on a flat casserole in one layer.

Purée or sieve the onion and liquid, and adjust seasoning – it may need more pepper, salt or sugar. Sugar is an essential flavour of this dish; it should be noticeable but not cloying.

Pour this sauce over the fish steaks.

Sprinkle with finely chopped walnuts.

Sole Florentine

Although Dover sole is the classic fish for this dish, it is rather expensive, and so I have often used plaice or even haddock, with excellent results. It is a very attractive dish, which can be prepared in advance and just grilled to be browned before serving.

Ingredients

700g sole or plaice (filleted)
1 lemon
2 tbs white wine, cider or water
½ onion
bay leaf
salt and pepper

Spinach purée

25g flour
25g butter
275ml milk
salt and pepper
500g fresh spinach (or 250g frozen spinach)

Béchamel sauce

25g butter
25g flour
150ml milk
1 clove garlic, crushed (optional)
salt and pepper

Topping

50g strong cheese, grated
2 tbs dried breadcrumbs
50g butter, melted

Method

Pre-heat oven to 180°C / gas mark 4.

Season and roll up the fish fillet.

Put fish in a casserole with chopped onion, lemon juice, wine, bay leaf, and seasoning.

Cover and bake for approximately 20 minutes. (This could be done in the microwave instead for speed.)

Put the washed spinach into a pan (no need to add water), and cook until wilted.

Finely chop wilted spinach. (If using chopped frozen spinach, just defrost.)

Make roux in another pan, i.e. melt butter, add flour, stir and cook until golden, then add milk gradually, then crushed garlic.

Add spinach and beat until the roux is well incorporated. Taste for seasoning.

To make béchamel sauce:

Melt butter, add flour and cook until blended.

Add milk and any liquid from the cooked fish.

Add garlic, if using.

Beat well to remove any lumps, and season to taste.

To assemble:

Put the spinach purée into the centre of a flat, ovenproof dish.

Arrange the cooked fish on top.

Cover the fish with béchamel sauce. Sprinkle with breadcrumbs, cheese, and melted butter.

Grill until brown and crisp.

Tip

If you use a larger dish, mashed potato can be piped or spooned around the outside, and grilled for a perfect finish.

Salmon Cutlets
(Using tinned pink or red salmon)

This is a store-cupboard recipe which I have found invaluable for impromptu picnics or unexpected visitors.

Ingredients *(Makes about 8 patties, or more smaller ones for picnics)*
   1 large tin salmon (about 400g)
   1 medium onion
   1 large or 2 small eggs
   3 tbs matzo meal or dry breadcrumbs
   1 tsp vinegar
   salt and pepper
   fine dry breadcrumbs (or matzo meal) for coating
   vegetable oil for frying

Method
   Chop onion and egg finely.

   Put salmon into large bowl, break up with fork.

   Add all other ingredients, and mix well. Taste for seasoning.

   Form into patties.

   Toss in breadcrumbs until well coated.

   Fry in hot oil until brown on both sides. Do not turn too soon – they will break.

   Drain on kitchen paper.

   Serve hot or cold.

Tip

If you have a food processor, the egg and onion can be whizzed together.

Fleisch — Meat

Healthy eating means less meat and more vegetables, fish and pulses. I shall therefore only include those meat recipes which are special to me. Some of these were the staples of my early years in Vienna, others I have collected over many years, but all have become family favourites.

Wiener Schnitzel –
Escalope of Pork or Turkey

Being Viennese, I cannot start with any dish other than the Wiener Schnitzel. Originally, if you ordered a Wiener Schnitzel in a restaurant or at a Gasthof, you were entitled to expect it to be made from best fillet of veal. Gradually it became known that you could make a very decent version by using fillet of pork, and nowadays restaurants in Austria often state Wiener Schnitzel 'vom Schwein' (made of pork). In Britain veal is not easy to obtain, so I use fillet of pork or, when dietary or health needs require it, chicken or turkey fillets.

It is simple to make. Basically, it is a piece of good quality meat, beaten very thin (with a special meat mallet, but the end of a rolling pin will do), coated with egg and breadcrumbs, and shallow fried. Any self-respecting Schnitzel should cover the plate. To a true Austrian, it is criminal to see a Schnitzel served with gravy, or decorated with olives, hard-boiled eggs, cheese, or any other trendy item. All a Schnitzel needs in the way of adornment is a slice of lemon.

Ingredients

500g pork fillet (cut into thin slices or escalopes, gristle removed)
flour to coat
1 beaten egg
1 bowl of dried breadcrumbs
salt
oil for shallow frying

Method

Beat escalopes well. (If using chicken, do this between clingfilm.)

Sprinkle each piece with salt.

With a sharp knife or scissors, make a few incisions all round the edge. (This keeps it flat during frying.)

Put a handful of flour onto a sheet of kitchen paper, and a bowlful of breadcrumbs onto a separate sheet.

Put the beaten egg into a soup plate, adding a little salt, and 1 tbs water.

Dip each escalope first into flour until coated, then into the egg mixture, and finally into the breadcrumbs.

Fry in hot oil until golden brown on both sides.

Drain on kitchen paper and serve as soon as possible.

Tip

The ideal accompaniment to Schnitzel is boiled new potatoes with parsley, or sautéed potatoes, and salads dressed with vinaigrette.

Leberschnitzel – Fried Liver

Offal is not used much these days, which is rather sad because it is a cheap and excellent source of protein. Cooked in this way it is crisp and tasty, and when accompanied by potatoes and a mixed salad makes a satisfying meal.

Ingredients

250g liver (ideally calf's, but it can be pig's or lamb's), cut into thin slices
milk for soaking
flour to coat
1 beaten egg
1 bowl of dried breadcrumbs
salt
oil for shallow frying

Method

Soak liver in milk for 10 minutes.

Dry on kitchen paper.

Proceed as for Wiener Schnitzel.

Naturschnitzel – Pork or Turkey with Mushrooms

A light and quickly prepared dish which can be eaten straight from the frying pan, but it can also be casseroled, which makes it ideal for entertaining.

Ingredients

450g thin slices of pork (tenderloin or thin pork chops)
  or slices of turkey breast
1 dsp flour
½ tsp paprika
1 crushed clove of garlic
½ tsp caraway seeds
150ml water or stock
1 tbs corn oil
125g button mushrooms
salt and pepper

Method

Mix paprika with flour, seasoning and caraway seeds.

Coat slices of meat with this mixture.

Heat oil in frying pan.

When hot, add meat. Fry for 5 minutes, then turn and cook for a further 5 minutes. Then remove from pan.

Add mushrooms to pan with a further dash of oil (or butter).

Season and fry for 3 minutes. Put on top of meat.

Add 1 dsp flour to the pan.

Scrape up the residue and add stock.

Cook until sauce thickens. Season to taste.

Pour over meat and mushrooms.

This can be served immediately, or refrigerated and reheated in the oven, in a covered casserole, at 175°C / gas mark 4 for approximately 30 minutes.

Serve on flat platter, surrounded by creamed potatoes, rice, or couscous.

Geröstete Nierndln – Kidneys with Onions

Ingredients

250g kidneys (pig or lamb)
1 large onion
1 dsp oil
1 dsp flour
1 tsp tomato purée
1 tsp sweet paprika
pepper
milk for soaking

Method

Soak kidneys in milk for at least 30 minutes. (This removes any bitter flavour.)

Dry on kitchen paper.

Cut into thin slices.

Chop onion, and fry in hot oil until golden.

Add kidneys. Increase heat, and toss kidneys until they change colour.

Add paprika, tomato purée, pepper, and flour. Stir well.

Add 150ml water, which will turn the mixture into a very tasty gravy.

Add salt and serve as soon as possible, as offal hardens if kept warm.

Tip

Do not add salt until the dish is complete, as salt hardens the kidneys.

Geröstete Leber – Austrian-style Liver and Onions

Ingredients

250g pig's or ox liver
1 large onion
1 dsp oil
1 dsp flour
1 tsp tomato purée
1 tsp sweet paprika
salt and pepper
milk for soaking

Method

Remove any green tinge and gristle from the liver, then proceed exactly as in the previous recipe.

Barbecue-style Roast Leg of Lamb

Most of the meat recipes given in this book are Austrian. Although I assume lamb and mutton are not entirely banned from Austrian kitchens, I am not aware of any Austrian recipes for using them. On the other hand, my family and friends make no secret of loving good roast lamb, so here is how I cook it.

Ingredients *(Serves 4–6 people)*
   1½ – 2kg leg of lamb (or lean shoulder)
   2 tbs oil
   1 tbs flour
   2 crushed cloves garlic
   1 tsp arrowroot

Dry marinade
   1 tsp salt
   1 tsp dry mustard
   1 tsp sugar
   ½ tsp pepper
   ½ tsp dry ginger

Sauce
   2 tbs tomato ketchup
   2 tbs Worcester sauce
   1 tbs redcurrant jelly
   dash of vinegar
   dash of Tabasco sauce
   350ml stock

Method
   Mix dry ingredients and rub into joint, then refrigerate overnight.

   Pre-heat the oven to 190°C / gas mark 5. Approximate roasting time is 25 minutes per 450g.

   Remove lamb from fridge, rub in garlic, dredge with flour.

   Heat oil in roasting tin on a gas or electric ring, and brown joint all over.

   Baste and put in oven to roast, basting at intervals.

Mix together all sauce ingredients.

After 1 hour take lamb from the oven, pour off fat, spoon half the sauce over the joint, then roast for a further 15 minutes.

Test to see if meat is cooked by inserting skewer into the thickest part. The juices which run out should be pink. If you prefer your meat more well cooked, leave for a further 20–30 minutes.

Put meat on a plate, cover and keep warm.

Pour off any excess fat from the residue in the roasting tin. Add remaining sauce and stir well.

Boil fast to evaporate sauce until halved in quantity.

Mix arrowroot with a little water, and add to the sauce to thicken it.

Gulasch / Rindsgulasch – Beef Stew

Gulyas is a Hungarian national dish. It is a soup. *Gulasch* is a very popular Austrian dish which is decidedly not a soup, but the two dishes have one important ingredient in common: sweet paprika, a Hungarian speciality. It is important to remember that you can also buy a very sharp paprika, not unlike chilli powder, which, if used in the same quantity as in this recipe, will make the dish almost inedible. In Austrian restaurants Gulasch is always available, often in either small or large portions, and makes an excellent choice if you like well-seasoned food.

I suspect the chefs often add a dash of beer, and although it is always served as the fresh dish of the day ('das Menü'), it really is better for being reheated, since the flavours have been allowed to develop. As long as it is refrigerated as soon as possible after cooking, and then reheated to a high temperature, this is a perfectly safe method and makes for very easy entertaining.

There are many variants: spicy sausage can be added, or Frankfurters cut into slices. An indispensable part of this dish is the rich, dark gravy. Indeed, if there is more gravy than needed, the left-overs make an excellent light meal served with a pair of Frankfurters, which is then known as 'Würstel mit Saft' – sausages with gravy.

There is even a version called Erdäpfelgulasch (potato goulash) without meat – ideal for your vegetarian guest (see 'Vegetables' chapter).

Ingredients *(For ordinary Gulasch)*

    500g lean stewing steak – shin, skirt or shoulder – cut
        into 2–3cm cubes
    500g onions, chopped
    1 level tbs sweet paprika
    1 tbs oil
    1 tbs tomato purée (optional)
    salt and pepper
    ¼ tsp caraway seeds
    1 tsp vinegar

Method

Heat oil. Add onions and fry until brown – the darker the colour the better the flavour.

Add meat and stir until it changes colour.

Add paprika.

Add all other ingredients and 2 tbs of water (or stock, wine or beer).

Simmer gently until the meat is tender. Keep a close watch not to let it boil dry, but only add a little liquid at a time.

When the meat is tender, adjust seasoning and add vinegar, and a little more liquid to increase the amount of gravy.

To thicken the gravy slightly, mix 1 dsp flour with a little cold water, and stir it into the Gulasch.

Serve with Nockerln (page 100), or plain boiled potatoes sprinkled with parsley, or pasta.

Gedünstetes Rindfleisch – Braised Beef

This is a good way of cooking beef slowly, ensuring that the finished dish is not only tasty, but also succulent. The secret is in seasoning it well, frying it quickly to seal in the juices, and then slowly simmering it. There is a small amount of liquid – it can be red wine or stock – which is added gradually. The meat must not be allowed to get dry. Braised brisket is delicious provided it is cooked very slowly, and it produces an excellent sauce.

Ingredients

1kg of lean brisket or silverside or topside of beef
2 tbs oil
2 cloves garlic, crushed
French or German mustard
salt and pepper
1 small onion
1 stalk of celery, roughly chopped
1 bay leaf
½ cup water or red wine
1 tsp cornflour to mix with 2 tbs water or wine

Method

Pre-heat the oven to 150°C / gas mark 2.

Brush the meat with mustard, rub all over with crushed garlic and season well.

Heat the oil in an ovenproof casserole or frying pan until really hot.

Fry the meat all round until brown.

Put into a casserole with a well-fitting lid.

Add vegetables and liquid, and cover.

Cook for approximately 2–3 hours. (Less time is needed for topside.)

Test with skewer for softness.

To serve, cut into slices and keep meat warm whilst making the sauce.

To make the sauce:

Push all the vegetables and liquid through a sieve (or blend in a blender).

Put into a small saucepan, skim off any fat and bring to the boil.

Mix 1 tsp cornflour with 2 tbs water or wine. Add this to the liquid to thicken. Taste for seasoning.

Pour some of the sauce over the sliced meat and serve the rest in a sauce boat.

Tip

It is a good idea to cook this joint a day before you want to serve it.
The meat will cut more easily when cold, and the fat will solidify on top and can easily be removed. Arrange slices neatly on a heatproof serving platter, cover and reheat with some of the sauce, serving the rest of the sauce in a sauce boat.

Sauerbraten – Marinaded Beef

This is specially flavoured meat which, because it is marinaded, will be tender even though it starts as a rather tough cut. Planning ahead is essential: the marinading takes 4 days.

Ingredients

1kg beef (silverside or very lean brisket) in 1 piece
2 tbs oil
2 cloves of garlic, crushed
1 tsp mustard (German or French)
¼ tsp mixed spice
salt and pepper
1 tsp arrowroot
150ml sour cream or crème fraîche

Marinade

1 onion, chopped
1 carrot, sliced
handful of parsley
1 stick of celery, chopped
1 bay leaf
200ml dry wine or beer

Method

Mix together all marinade ingredients.

Put meat into suitable dish, cover with marinade, soak for 4 days in fridge, turning daily in marinade.

After 4 days, lift the meat from the marinade and pat dry.

Drain the vegetables, reserving the marinade.

Cut slits into the meat with a sharp knife, and insert slivers of garlic.

Rub in mustard and seasoning.

Heat oil in heavy casserole and brown the meat all round. Remove.

Brown vegetables in same casserole, put meat on top.

Pour 150ml marinade over.

Bake in oven at 160°C / gas mark 2–3 for approximately 2 hours.

Remove meat and allow to cool a little before slicing.

Strain gravy, put into a small pan, de-grease then thicken with arrowroot which has been combined with the sour cream or crème fraîche.

Stir until it thickens.

Adjust seasoning to taste.

Pour a little over the sliced meat, serving the rest separately.

Faschierter Braten (Hackbraten) – Minced Loaf Roast

Minced beef dishes are very popular in Austria. As a child I always preferred a minced beef loaf or 'beefburger' to fillet steak.

As a new housewife after the war, when meat was still rationed, I was fortunate in having experienced my mother's ingenuity in managing to make miraculous meals for any number of people using limited supplies of minced meat. She could always 'stretch' it by adding a bit more bread to the mixture, or increasing the amount of sauce to go with it. It gives me real pleasure to be able to share my mother's recipes with you.

Basic Mixture

Choose your meat carefully. I like to get my meat freshly minced and, although it's a little more expensive, I buy shoulder steak.

Ingredients
500g minced shoulder steak
1 level tsp salt
1 egg
1 medium onion, finely chopped
1 thick slice of bread, soaked in water and squeezed dry
freshly ground pepper

Method
Put the meat into a dish, add all other ingredients, and mix. I like to use my hands to get a really good mixture, but egg, onion and bread can be mixed in a food processor for speed.

To make into a minced roast loaf
Pre-heat oven to 190°C / gas mark 5.
Shape the mixture into an oblong 'sausage' approximately 8cm x 17cm.
Sprinkle lightly with some breadcrumbs or crushed cornflakes.
Drizzle with a little olive oil.
Roast for 1 hour, basting occasionally.

When cooked, remove the loaf and keep warm. The residue in the baking tin will make an excellent gravy.

Add 1 dsp flour to any fat/meat juices, and stir over a gentle heat until juices are absorbed, and the flour is golden brown.

Add 150ml vegetable stock or water, stirring to mix, and adjust seasoning to taste.

Tip

This roast is equally good eaten cold, in slices with a salad or as a picnic food. To make it a bit special, take 2 hard-boiled eggs and encase them in above meat mixture before roasting.

Faschierte Laberln – Beefburgers

I hope I won't be sued if I admit that when I made these for my youngest grandson we called them McSchatzis!

Ingredients

1 quantity of basic minced meat mixture
2 tbs flour
1 egg, beaten and seasoned with salt and pepper
4 tbs dried breadcrumbs
oil for frying

Method

Shape basic mixture into 8 patties.

Cover and refrigerate for 30 minutes to firm up.

Coat patties first in flour, then in beaten egg, and finally in breadcrumbs.

Fry in hot, shallow oil until golden brown on both sides.

Tip

----

*For a lower calorie version, omit the egg and breadcrumb coating,
brush lightly with olive oil, and grill on both sides for about 8 minutes.*

Gefülltes Kraut – Stuffed Cabbage Leaves

This is a popular recipe cooked in many countries in Europe, the Middle East, and elsewhere. It is known by different names, and a variety of ingredients are used, according to local custom. The following recipe is our favourite. It can be made in advance, freezes and reheats well, and is ideal for economical entertaining.

Ingredients

    1 white cabbage, tough outer leaves removed

Stuffing

    250g minced beef
    1 small onion, chopped
    3 tbs boiled rice
    ½ tsp salt
    pepper

Sauce

    150g tin of tomato purée
    250ml water
    2 tbs lemon juice
    2 tbs brown sugar

Method

Pre-heat the oven to 150°C / gas mark 2.

Take 8 leaves of cabbage and soak in boiling water for about 10 minutes.

Drain the cabbage leaves, cut away the hard centre stem.

Mix stuffing ingredients to a firm paste.

Put equal amounts into each of the cabbage leaves and roll up tightly, turning the ends in.

Put cabbage rolls close together (to avoid unrolling) in a suitable ovenproof dish.

Mix sauce ingredients together, add salt and pepper to taste and pour over the rolls.

Cover the dish with a lid or foil.

Cook in oven for 2 hours, then uncover, increase heat to 200°C / gas mark 6 and cook until sauce thickens, and rolls are brown on top.

Serve with boiled, preferably new, potatoes.

Gefüllte Paprika in Paradeissauce – Stuffed Peppers in Tomato Sauce

Use the same meat mixture as given in the recipe for stuffed cabbage leaves (page 71). The rice can be replaced by soaked bread.

Ingredients

250g mixture of minced beef (or half pork / half beef),
    as for stuffed cabbage leaves
4 medium-sized green peppers

Sauce

1 tbs oil or butter
1 tbs flour
150g tin tomato purée
275ml stock or water
1 tsp sugar
1 tsp lemon juice
salt and pepper

Method

Slice tops off the peppers, reserving to use as lids.

Remove all the seeds, then wash empty peppers.

Fill with stuffing, and cover with 'lid'.

Sauce

Melt butter or heat oil in a large saucepan.

Add flour, and cook until golden.

Gradually add stock. Beat sauce to remove lumps.

Add tomato purée, seasoning, lemon juice, and sugar. Stir until sauce is smooth.

Place stuffed peppers in the sauce. Cover, and simmer slowly for approximately 1 hour.

Stir occasionally, ensuring that the sauce does not evaporate or burn.

Serve with plain boiled potatoes.

See overleaf for tip

Tip

---

*I find that this dish is far better cooked slowly on top of the stove.
If done in the oven, the sauce gets too thin.*

Paprika Huhn – Chicken Paprika

Although chicken is no longer the luxury item it once was, we still regard it as a special weekly event, and I try to plan the menu around it to make it that bit special. We usually start the meal with chicken soup (page 18), served with a freshly baked challah (plaited loaf of bread – page 196). My method of cooking the bird depends on its quality. The better the chicken, the simpler the recipe, as I like to let the flavour speak for itself. A plain roasted chicken hardly needs explaining, but the two variants given here will add interest to an ordinary bird.

Ingredients

1 roasting chicken (cut into 4–6 portions)
225g onions, chopped
2 tbs oil
1 tbs flour, seasoned with 1 tsp paprika and salt and pepper
1 green or red pepper
1 tbs tomato purée
2 rashers of smoked bacon
150ml stock or wine
1 tbs vinegar
150mg sour cream or crème fraîche (optional)

Method

Pre-heat oven to 180°C / gas mark 4.

Coat chicken pieces in seasoned flour.

Dice bacon, and slice green or red pepper.

Fry diced bacon in heavy casserole. Remove.

Add oil, fry onions and sliced pepper.

Fry chicken until brown. Add the above ingredients to the fried chicken.

Add wine or stock and tomato purée. Cover and cook in oven for approximately 1 hour. Taste for seasoning. Add dash of vinegar.

Stir in the sour cream, adjust seasoning, and serve with rice, pasta, or polenta.

Tip

Do not re-boil once cream has been added.

Backhuhn – Oven-baked Chicken

This is a big favourite in Austria, particularly at the Heurigen. A Heuriger is a cross between a bistro and a gastro-pub, often offering live traditional music (accordion, violin, guitar, clarinet, in any combination) to create a magical atmosphere. 'Heuriger' literally means 'this season's new wine', which tastes light but is deceptively strong. Ideally consumed in the open air, the wine is accompanied by food, music and chat. Tables are laden with all sorts of specialities, one of which is invariably the famous 'Backhendl' (as Backhuhn is known in Vienna).

The original recipe calls for deep frying. I have adjusted this to the oven-baked version, which is not only healthier, but also easier to cook, and the result is equally good.

Ingredients

1 chicken, cut into 6 portions (do not remove skin)

Coating

2 egg yolks
3 tbs oil
salt and pepper
dry breadcrumbs

Method

Pre-heat oven to 190°C / gas mark 5.

Beat yolks and oil.

Place crumbs, seasoned with salt and pepper, on kitchen paper.

Dip chicken into oil mixture, using a pastry brush to ensure that pieces are covered.

Press crumbs well onto each piece.

Put chicken on a shallow baking tray and place in hot oven for 30 minutes, then turn each piece, and continue until both sides are evenly brown and crisp.

Serve with a mixed green salad or potato salad.

Hungarian Shoulder of Lamb

This recipe should really be made with shoulder of veal, or breast of veal, but as veal is hardly obtainable in this country and is generally frowned upon, I have converted it to be used with lamb – a very good alternative.

Ingredients

1 medium-sized shoulder of lamb
  (boned – ask your butcher to bone it)
2 cloves of garlic
1 tsp sweet paprika
½ tsp salt
¼ tsp pepper
50g butter (or soft margarine)
1 shallot (or small onion)
150ml stock
3 tomatoes
2 halves of canned pimentos
1 tbs flour
2–3 tbs sour cream or Greek yoghurt

Method

Pre-heat oven to 190°C / gas mark 5.

Crush garlic. Beat together with butter, seasoning and paprika.

Open up the boned meat, put half the butter mixture in it, roll up and tie with string.

Make incisions into meat, and rub in remainder of butter mixture.

Heat 1 dsp oil in roasting tin.

Add meat, baste with hot oil. Put in oven for approximately 1 hour and 30 minutes (or 20 minutes per 450g plus an extra 20 minutes), basting every 15 minutes.

Peel tomatoes, first plunging them into boiling water for 5 minutes to loosen skins.

Slice tomatoes and pimento.

When meat is cooked (test with skewer; liquid should come out clear), remove and keep warm.

Pour excess fat from tin, add flour, stir until brown.

Add stock, stir until smooth, add slices of tomato and pimento. Bring to boil.

Cut meat into generous slices. Pour the sauce over the meat.

Spoon the sour cream over the middle of the slices.

Cover with foil and reheat in oven for a further 10 minutes.

Serve with roasted potatoes and vegetables of your choice.

Gemüse – Vegetables

Not only are vegetables a nutritionally important part of our diet, but also there is nothing better than very fresh vegetables, cooked 'al dente' and served with a little butter. However, it is not always possible to buy the freshest of vegetables, and since it also adds interest to a meal to serve something a little different, I have included some recipes from store cupboard ingredients. You may find these useful for busy or wintry days.

Some of the recipes in this chapter make good vegetarian main course dishes. More can be found in the 'Pasta and Dumplings' chapter.

Schwammerl Schnitzel – Mushroom Escalopes (V)

During my childhood there was quite an epidemic of Scarlet Fever, and true to form I contracted the disease, which had to be taken very seriously. My mother had to give me a meat-free diet for several weeks. This was my introduction to this splendid dish, and I have since used it for the vegetarians in the family. It tastes surprisingly meaty and satisfying, and is an ideal substitute for meat.

Ingredients

large flat mushrooms (2 or 3 per person)
coating exactly as for Schnitzel (see page 54)
salt and pepper
oil for shallow frying

Method

Wash mushrooms (no need to peel them).

Dry on paper towel.

Season with salt and pepper. A little crushed garlic could be added.

Coat with Schnitzel coating.

Fry in hot oil until golden brown.

Drain on kitchen paper and serve, accompanied by potatoes, salads or vegetables.

Kartoffelgulasch / Erdäpfelgulasch – Potato Stew (V)

The Kartoffelgulasch of my childhood did not contain any carrots or chick-peas, and Marmite was not known. I have added these ingredients for the benefit of a more balanced diet. The additions are optional.

Ingredients

500g potatoes
300g onions
200g carrots
200g tinned chick-peas (or equivalent amount of soaked dried ones)
1 level tbs sweet paprika
1 tbs tomato purée
½ tsp Marmite
1 tbs oil
½ tsp caraway seeds
1 tsp vinegar
salt and pepper to taste
water or stock

Method

Heat oil in large pan.

Chop and fry onions until rich golden brown.

Peel potatoes and cut into chunks.

Peel and slice carrots.

Add all the ingredients and spices to the onions.

Add stock to almost cover the potatoes.

Simmer gently until everything is soft.

Stir to break up the potatoes. Add vinegar.

Adjust liquid and seasoning as necessary.

Karfiol mit Bröseln –
Cauliflower with Buttered Breadcrumbs (V)

This method of serving vegetables is quite common in Austria. Sprouts and asparagus are also often done in this way. It is not recommended for calorie counters, but tastes good and is a useful dish for vegetarians, who can add some grated cheese for extra flavour and protein. Incidentally, the word 'Karfiol' is only used in Austria. In Germany this vegetable is known as 'Blumenkohl' (literally, flower cabbage). In Vienna this dish is often regarded as a main meal, and served with either a substantial soup or pudding.

Ingredients

1 firm cauliflower
50g butter (or a healthy equivalent)
2 tbs dried breadcrumbs

Method

Boil cauliflower in plenty of salted water until just soft. (It is often boiled whole and looks attractive when served sprinkled with the buttered crumbs, but I prefer to break it up into large florets, including some of the green if it is really fresh. This way it is easier to keep 'al dente'.)

Whilst the cauliflower is boiling, melt the butter, add the dry breadcrumbs and fry until they are golden brown.

It is usual to serve this with melted butter poured on top which, for health reasons, I omit.

Spinat – Creamed Spinach (V)

This way of cooking either fresh or frozen spinach makes for a delicious vegetable, and is the basis for Eggs Florentine, as well as being an ideal accompaniment for salmon.

Ingredients

450g fresh spinach, or small packet of frozen spinach
25g butter or oil
1 dsp flour
1 fat clove of garlic, crushed
150ml milk (approximately)
salt and pepper

Method

Wash spinach, and put in pan without any further liquid. Boil until wilted.

Strain and squeeze dry. Chop roughly.

Melt butter. Add flour.

Stir until well blended.

Add garlic and seasoning.

Add milk gradually, beating the mixture to remove lumps.

Add spinach, and stir to get smooth consistency.

Eggs Florentine (V)

A fried or poached egg served on a bed of spinach purée as above, with new potatoes, is a simple and attractive meal. Use 1 egg per person.

Grüne Fisolen – French Beans (V)

There tends to be a glut of beans in summer, particularly for gardeners who grow their own. This rather different recipe makes a change to the plain boiled variety.

Ingredients

500g French beans
25g butter or oil
1 tbs flour
1 tsp sugar
1 tsp vinegar or lemon juice
salt and pepper

Method

String the beans. If large, cut into thin diagonal slices.

Cover with boiling water.

Add pinch of salt.

Cover, and cook until almost soft.

Make a roux with butter or oil and flour.

Stir until the roux is light brown.

Strain beans, reserving liquid.

Add enough liquid to roux to give the consistency of a thin sauce.

Add beans, vinegar or lemon juice and sugar.

Aim for a pleasant sweet-and-sour taste, seasoning with salt and pepper.

Rotkraut – Piquant Red Cabbage (V)

This vegetable is often served in restaurants now, but sadly it usually lacks that essential piquant taste which should characterise it. Red cabbage makes a very good accompaniment to any rich meat or poultry. It is ideal for Christmas entertaining as it can be made in advance. It is hardly worth making a small quantity, as it freezes well and will also keep in the fridge for a few days.

Ingredients

1 red cabbage, shredded
1 cooking apple, grated
1 onion, finely shredded
2 tbs sugar
1 tbs oil
1 tbs wine vinegar
salt and pepper
pinch of caraway seeds
1 clove, or a pinch of powdered cloves

Method

Heat the oil in a heavy pan.

Add sugar, allowing to brown just lightly.

Have the shredded vegetables ready, and tip them into the pan immediately.

Add all other ingredients except vinegar. Stir and cover. (Do not add any water. The cabbage must cook slowly in its own juice.)

Check at regular intervals to avoid burning. If the mixture gets too dry, add a very small amount of water.

Simmer for approximately 45 minutes. Add vinegar and adjust seasoning.

Cabbage should have a distinct sweet-and-sour taste.

It improves greatly by being reheated.

Tip

A little warning: when browning the sugar take care. One second it's a nice golden colour, and the next, it's burnt!

Gedünstetes Kraut –
Braised White Cabbage (V)

This readily available winter vegetable can be cooked in the same way as Rotkraut, and freezes equally well.

Ingredients

   1 firm white cabbage, shredded
   1 tbs sugar
   pinch caraway seeds
   salt and pepper
   1 onion, chopped
   1 tbs oil
   1 tbs wine vinegar
   1 tbs tomato purée (or concentrate, available in tubes)

Method

   Follow method for red cabbage.

Sauerkraut – Pickled Cabbage (V)

Before the era of frozen vegetables, Sauerkraut was a staple winter vegetable in Austria. It was pickled in big wooden barrels, and you bought great dollops of it.

I loved to nibble a little bit raw on the way home from the shop. It was reputedly a great cure for a hangover.

Sauerkraut is an excellent side dish with pork, ham and bacon, and is now available in supermarkets, usually in glass jars. My store cupboard is never without a jar of Sauerkraut and a tin of Frankfurters. But it does need cooking. I was once persuaded to have a sausage and Sauerkraut at a market stall in York, when the sausage was greasy and the Sauerkraut cold and raw. A chastening experience.

Ingredients

450g jar of Sauerkraut
water to cover
1 onion
1 dsp oil
2 medium potatoes
1 tsp tomato purée
½ tsp caraway seeds
pepper
sugar to taste (about 1 tsp)

Method

Put Sauerkraut into sieve. Rinse well to remove excess salt.

Chop onion, and fry in oil until soft.

Grate potatoes coarsely.

Add strained cabbage (Sauerkraut), potatoes, tomato purée, pepper, and caraway seeds.

Cover with water.

Simmer for approximately 45 minutes, stirring occasionally.

Taste, and add sugar as necessary.

Karotten und Erbsen – Carrots and Peas (V)

Many Continental vegetable dishes are served with their own sauce, this sometimes being referred to as 'dressed'. In Austria, the English method of boiling, or latterly steaming, vegetables and serving them plain or with a little butter is often referred to as 'healthy eating'. It is an excellent way with really fresh produce, but vegetables dressed in the Austrian way can bring variety to the menu. Fresh peas and young carrots make a wonderful spring accompaniment, but throughout the year almost the same results can be achieved with older carrots and frozen peas.

Ingredients

500g peeled carrots
500g fresh peas (shelled weight); frozen peas can also be used
25g butter
1 tsp sugar
1 cup water
1 dsp flour
chopped parsley
salt and pepper

Method

Melt butter in a saucepan. Add carrots and peas.

Sprinkle with sugar, and add seasoning.

Add water, and simmer until just tender.

Do not strain, but sprinkle flour on top.

Stir to blend in. This will create a light sauce.

Finish with chopped parsley.

Linsen – Brown or Green Lentils (V)

This is often regarded as an excellent winter dish when fresh vegetables are scarce, and it makes a good standby for vegetarians or unexpected guests. Brown and green lentils, less common in this country than red or yellow ones, are flavoursome, nutritious and do not require soaking. They are served in their own sauce, so are ideal as an accompaniment to food such as sausages (especially Frankfurters), ham, bacon, or just jacket potatoes.

Ingredients

225g brown or green lentils
1 tbs oil or margarine
1 tbs flour
1 dsp wine vinegar or lemon juice
2 tsp sugar
salt and pepper
1 bay leaf (optional)
water to cover

Method

Wash lentils thoroughly, and cover with water.

Add a pinch of salt (more is added at a later stage).

Bring to boil, and simmer until tender. This will take approximately 30 minutes.

Strain the liquid into a bowl. There should be about 1 cup of liquid left.

In a separate pan, melt the fat, add the flour, and stir until the flour changes colour.

Add the cooking liquid from the lentils. Stir well to get a smooth sauce.

Season with salt and pepper, and add vinegar and sugar. Stir the lentils into this sauce.

Add more water if consistency is too thick.

The taste should be distinctly sweet-and-sour, so adjust seasoning accordingly.

Kochsalat mit Erbsen – Lettuce and Peas (V)

For this unusual combination of vegetables you need a large cos lettuce. It is a good way of using all the large dark green leaves, which contain most of the vitamins, as well as the lighter internal leaves. This is a summer vegetable for the months when lettuce is plentiful. If you are a keen gardener you may well have an abundance in your garden.

Ingredients

1 large cos lettuce
500g fresh peas (shelled weight); frozen peas can also be used
1 medium-sized onion
1 clove garlic, crushed (optional)
salt and pepper
pinch of sugar
1 tbs flour
1 tbs butter
150ml milk

Method

Cut the lettuce into shreds. Add the peas, salt, pepper and sugar.

Add ½ cup of water, and cook until peas are tender.

Strain and reserve liquid for sauce.

Chop onion. Fry in butter until golden, then add crushed garlic (optional).

Add flour, stirring to coat onions.

Gradually add cooking liquid and milk, beating to remove any lumps.

Add the vegetables to the sauce.

Adjust seasoning to taste.

Potato Latkes (Jewish) / Kartoffelpuffer – Potato Cakes (V)

These delectable potato cakes originate from Russia and Poland. The original recipe was given to me by my boyfriend (later to become my husband) on a camping holiday. He remembered them from his childhood. He patiently shredded the potato with a penknife, and then we managed to cook them on a little camping stove.

Here is a much less labour-intensive method! Latkes are an excellent side dish to roast chicken, but good enough to eat on their own. For those watching their weight, the problem is that they are fried, and that they are really best eaten straight out of the frying pan.

We have bought similar versions in Germany, where they are often sold by street vendors with a dollop of apple purée. In Austria, the vendors sometimes cook them on the griddles used for roasting chestnuts, and these are not quite as successful.

Ingredients (*Makes 3 to 4 portions, depending on appetite*)

2 or 3 large potatoes (about 350g when grated)
1 egg
2 level tbs self-raising flour
½ tsp salt and some pepper
corn oil for shallow frying

Method

Peel and grate potatoes on coarse grater.

Put into a sieve. Leave to drain for 10 minutes, then squeeze out as much liquid as possible.

Potatoes tend to go brown, but in this case this does not matter.

Put into a bowl and add all other ingredients.

Pour about 1cm oil into a heavy frying pan and heat to a high temperature.

Put in a tablespoonful of the mixture at a time, flattening it with the back of the spoon.

Do not overcrowd the latkes in the pan.

Fry on medium heat until brown, then turn and fry other side.

Drain on crumpled kitchen paper, and serve as soon as possible.

Latkes can be kept warm, and can also be frozen and reheated, but at a cost – they will not taste as good as when fresh.

Tip

For the weight and health conscious, it's possible to achieve reasonable results with the oven-baked version below. Not as delectable as the fried version, but can be eaten guilt-free!

Potato Latkes – baked version

Method

Pre-heat the oven to 200°C / gas mark 6.

Oil a flat baking tray, and place in oven to get very hot.

For each latke, put 1 tbs mixture onto tray, then flatten.

Brush latkes with oil.

Bake for approximately 40 minutes, turning after 20 minutes. Latkes should be crisp and golden brown.

Geröste – Sautéed Potatoes (V)

These are Austria's answer to the more familiar Swiss Rösti delicacy, but are much simpler to make, and never fail to please.

Ingredients

500g potatoes (waxy ones are preferable to King Edwards)
1 tbs oil (pork or bacon dripping is the original ingredient)
1 onion (optional, but vital as far as my husband is concerned!)
salt and pepper

Method

Boil scrubbed potatoes in their skin in salted water until just soft.

Fry chopped onion in fat, using a heavy frying pan, until soft.

Peel potatoes. Cut into slices and add to onions. Season with pepper and salt.

Stir and leave to brown underneath, getting crusty.

An occasional stir is necessary.

The finished dish should not be mashed, but should have a crusty, speckled appearance.

Tip

If ever you make Schnitzels (see page 54), use the strained fat and crumb residue in the frying pan to make these potatoes. Saves a pan and adds flavour.

Gebratene Kartoffeln –
Glazed Jacket Potatoes with Caraway (V)

This is such a simple version of a popular dish that I am surprised nobody seems to know about it. My mother had a small shop in Vienna, and I used to go there after school. In winter the little coke-burning stove in the corner was lit, and there was usually a treat for me on the flat top. It was either a potato baked in the following way, or a baked apple – sometimes even both.

Ingredients

large well-scrubbed potatoes, 1 per person
a few caraway seeds
sea salt

Method

Pre-heat oven to 200°C / gas mark 6.

Cut raw potatoes in half. Sprinkle with caraway seeds and coarse sea salt.

Bake with sprinkled side up for approximately 40 minutes.

The cooked potatoes finish with a glossy golden hue, taste delicious and cook in half the time a whole potato would take.

Rice

There are a great many different types of rice, a staple food used not only in Eastern countries, but also in the Western world. I will limit myself to describing the four main types.

Patna Rice: a good rice for general use, long grains which stay separate when boiled.

Basmati Rice: a more delicate rice with a very aromatic flavour, predominantly used in Indian cooking.

Carolina Rice: a small grain which readily absorbs a large amount of liquid, ideal for rice puddings when a glutinous consistency is required.

Italian (Arborio) Rice: used for risotto, gives creamy consistency but maintains a certain chewiness.

Quantities: as with pasta, one is tempted to cook more than necessary! A good guide is approximately 40g per portion, or a medium-sized cup for two portions.

During my childhood, rice came to the retailer (they were called grocers in those days) in large hessian sacks, the grocer then having to weigh it out. It was not cleaned and I used to help my mother pick out little stones and other bits before washing the rice thoroughly. Nowadays, rice comes ready cleaned and is also often washed. Many recipes, however, tell you to wash the rice until the water runs clear, in order to get rid of excess starch. Having tried various different techniques for obtaining fluffy and separate grains, I give here the recipe which never fails for me.

Plain Boiled Rice (V)

Ingredients

1 cup Patna or Basmati rice
2 cups boiling water
1 level tsp salt
1 tbs oil

Method

Melt oil in large frying pan.

Add rice. Stir until all grains are coated with oil.

Add boiling water and bring to boil.

Cover with lid, turn down heat and leave to simmer slowly for approximately 20 minutes.

When liquid is absorbed and grains are soft, remove from heat.

To keep warm, put a tea towel over pan and put lid on top of tea towel.

Leave for a further few minutes. The tea towel will absorb the steam.

Fluff up gently with a fork.

Tip

If chilled immediately after cooking, rice reheats well the following day in either the microwave or the oven. It also freezes well, so if there is any left over it can be used later to add to savoury stuffings, stir-fries etc.

Rice with Peas (Risi-Pisi) (V)

Boil rice according to instructions given in previous recipe.
When cooked, add 1 cup of de-frosted frozen peas.
Add a little oil or butter.

Rice with Beans (V)

As the previous recipe, but use a small tin of drained haricot beans instead of peas.

Nudeln und Knödeln –
Pasta and Dumplings

The word 'pasta' is normally associated with Italian food, but pasta dough is, in fact, frequently used in Austrian cuisine. The Italian Tyrol, now on Austria's southern border, was once part of the Austro-Hungarian Empire. Whether the common use of pasta in Austria is a result of this proximity, or whether the Austrians would have given it the relatively prominent place in its diet anyway, is a moot point.

When I was a child in Vienna, no self-respecting housewife would buy ready-made pasta. I vividly remember my mother mixing the dough, not in a bowl, but on a special wooden board called the Nudelbrett (noodleboard). After a lot of kneading, the dough was rolled into large sheets which were hung on the edge of the kitchen table to become semi-dry. Only then could they be cut into strips, either to make very thin noodles, the thicker tagliatelle type, or little squares ('Fleckerln').

Though it is fun to try, and educative for our children to see how these things are made, the availability of good pasta makes this laborious exercise unnecessary. I wonder how many pasta machines are languishing in various kitchen cupboards without ever being used!

Nockerln – Gnocchi (V)

These are often served as accompaniment to Gulasch, but can also be delicious without meat.

Ingredients

225g plain flour
½ tsp salt
1 egg
275ml milk
1 dsp oil
large pan of salted boiling water

Method

Sift flour and salt together.

Add egg and gradually beat in the milk. Consistency should be that of a very thick paste.

To shape these little oblong pastas, dip a dessertspoon into the boiling water, put a small amount of paste on its tip, and slip that into the boiling water.

Repeat until the paste is used up. (Speed comes with practice. If you are daring, you can put the paste onto a small board and, with a knife, snip little bits into the boiling liquid. This is quicker, and is the method chefs and experienced cooks use. You can even buy a special board for the purpose, called a Nockerlbrett, but that would probably necessitate a trip to Austria.)

Boil for approximately 5 minutes, until the Nockerln float on top.

Strain into a sieve, serving straight away if used as an accompaniment.

If they are to be eaten a little later, rinse them in cold water and, when ready to reheat, toss them with a little hot butter or oil in a frying pan.

Eiernockerln – Pasta with Eggs (V)

The previous recipe can be turned into a tasty and healthy meal, often served in summer. It's also a useful standby when the cupboard is almost bare.

Ingredients

1 quantity of prepared Nockerln (see previous recipe)
3 or 4 eggs
1 tbs butter or oil
salt and pepper

Method

Heat butter or oil in a frying pan.

Put the Nockerln into pan, add the beaten, seasoned eggs and stir, rather like making scrambled eggs.

Serve straight away with cucumber salad, or a mixed green salad.

Serviettenknödeln – Savoury Dumplings (V)

Dumplings are very popular not only in Austria, but also in the areas of Europe which were once part of the Austro-Hungarian Empire. They come in all sizes, from tiny ones which are used as garnish for soups, to larger ones described below. There is an extensive variety of sweet dumplings (see 'Puddings and Desserts' chapter), and the only thing they have in common is the round shape. And even that is not the case with Serviettenknödeln, which are 'Knödel' only because of their content, not their shape.

Ingredients

200g stale white bread, cut into 1cm cubes
1 egg
150ml milk
salt and pepper
chopped parsley

Method

Mix together egg, seasoning and milk.

Pour over cubed bread. Leave to soak for 2 hours.

Form into a thick sausage.

Loosely wrap in muslin, or a tea towel (hence the name 'Servietten' – napkins).

Immerse in a pan of boiling water.

Boil gently for 35 minutes.

Remove from pan, unwrap, cut into thickish slices, and serve as a side dish with Sauerkraut, mushroom sauce, etc.

Semmelknödeln – Bread Dumplings (V)

Similar to Serviettenknödeln, but made into individual dumplings. Any size between a golf ball and a tennis ball will do. Often served as an alternative side dish to potatoes.

Ingredients
4 thick slices of white bread
1 tbs oil (the traditional fat used is pork dripping)
1 egg
1 cup of milk
100g plain flour
salt and pepper

Method
Cut bread into 1cm cubes.

Heat oil in frying pan. Add bread cubes and fry until golden.

Sift flour and add seasoning.

Add egg and milk, beating until smooth (aim for a thick batter consistency).

Add fried bread cubes.

Leave to stand for 30 minutes.

Wet hands, and form dumplings. If mixture is too soft, add more plain flour until it is mouldable.

Bring a large pan of water to the boil, add 1 tsp salt, immerse dumplings.

Boil for approximately 10 minutes, until they float on top. Strain.

To avoid them sticking together, toss in a little oil or butter.

Keep warm and serve.

Tip

Any left-over dumplings can be turned into a tasty supper or lunch dish called Knödel mit Ei – see the next recipe.

Knödel mit Ei –
Dumpling with Scrambled Egg (V)

Ingredients

left-over dumplings (see previous recipe)
1 tbs oil or butter
2 eggs, beaten and seasoned with salt and pepper

Method

Cut dumplings into small slices.

Melt oil or butter in a frying pan.

Add dumpling pieces, and stir until hot (they will go slightly crisp).

Add seasoned beaten eggs, stirring until dumplings are coated with scrambled egg, and serve, preferably with a tossed green salad.

Spinach Pancakes (V)

This is my way of creating a dish which is a bit like cannelloni. I find it far easier to use pancakes than the authentic egg dough tubes, and I have tried a variety of methods. So, you might like to try this cheat's version of cannelloni.

Use 12 ready-cooked pancakes (see pancake recipe, page 140).

Ingredients

Spinach filling
- 250g of fresh spinach or a small packet of frozen spinach
- 25g butter or margarine
- 1 clove garlic, crushed, or a little ground nutmeg
- 1 boiled potato or 1 tbs breadcrumbs
- salt and pepper

Cheese sauce
- 25g butter or 1 tbs olive oil
- 25g flour
- ½ tsp dried mustard
- salt and pepper
- 275ml milk
- 50g strong grated cheese (parmesan if available, or a mixture of cheeses)

Method

Butter a suitable small-ish casserole to allow the pancakes to fit snugly.

Wash fresh spinach. Cook in a saucepan without extra water until wilted.

Squeeze well to remove any liquid. If using frozen spinach, simply drain well.

Add all other ingredients.

Fill each pancake with this mixture, roll up, tuck sides underneath.

Put them closely together to avoid unrolling.

To make cheese sauce
    Melt butter or heat oil.
    Add flour and mustard, and stir until well blended.
    Add milk gradually, beating well to make a smooth mixture.
    Add cheese, but reserve 1 tbs for sprinkling on top.
    Pour sauce over pancakes, then sprinkle with cheese.

    Place under a hot grill until golden brown and bubbling.
    Decorate finished dish with thin slices of tomato.

Tip

A balloon whisk helps to make the cheese sauce really smooth.

Schinkenfleckerln – Pasta with Ham or Bacon

Though I've searched long and hard for them, it seems that Fleckerln (pasta squares, approximately 1cm), which are as easily available in Austria as tagliatelle are in Britain, are unobtainable here. But the dishes described can be made using broken tagliatelle, and you would not know the difference. Judging the amount of pasta needed is always a bit difficult, and even the most experienced cook is sometimes left with too much. A general rule is about 60g per person.

This is an excellent, economical dish which can be stretched according to the number of guests; quantities can be flexible. I have even used corned beef instead of ham, or the remains of a ham shank.

There used to be a popular hit song in Vienna which had a refrain 'Why is it that the ham always plays hide-and-seek with the Fleckerln?'

Ingredients

250g dried tagliatelle
150g cooked bacon or ham (more if you feel generous)
2 eggs, separated
1 tbs margarine or oil
25g grated cheese
1 tbs dried breadcrumbs
a little butter

Method

Break up tagliatelle by putting them in a strong plastic bag and beating them with a rolling pin or mallet.

Boil broken pasta in plenty of salted water until 'al dente'. Rinse.

Put into mixing bowl. Add fat, ham, egg yolks, freshly ground pepper, and salt.

Beat egg whites and fold into mixture in bowl.

Grease an ovenproof casserole, put pasta mixture in casserole.

Sprinkle with cheese, and top with breadcrumbs. Add a few flakes of butter.

Bake at 175°C / gas mark 3 for approximately 30 minutes until golden brown.

Serve with a green crisp salad dressed with vinaigrette.

Krautfleckerln – Pasta with Cabbage (V)

A vegetarian version of the above recipe is tagliatelle with braised cabbage. The same amount of pasta is mixed with the cooked cabbage (see recipe on page 86). It needs little accompaniment, but is attractive if garnished with tomato slices.

Pasta Salad (V)

This is a simple and substantial salad, and can be altered according to taste with a variety of different ingredients. It is a good way of using left-overs such as chicken or ham, but fresh pineapple or grapes are good alternatives.

Ingredients

225g pasta bows or shells
3 medium carrots, peeled and coarsely grated
1 or 2 unpeeled eating apples, chopped
1 tbs lemon juice
1 heaped tbs sultanas, soaked in hot water and drained
2 tbs mayonnaise and 2 tbs yoghurt, or 4 tbs mayonnaise
salt and pepper
watercress (for garnish)

Method

Boil pasta following packet instructions.

Add lemon juice to chopped apple to prevent discoloration.

Mix all ingredients.

Serve on a flat platter, surrounded with watercress.

Käsenudeln – Noodle and Cheese Bake (V)

Ingredients

175g egg tagliatelle
150ml sour cream or Greek yoghurt
225g carton Quark/curd cheese or sifted cottage cheese
2 eggs
chopped spring onions
1 tbs butter

Method

Boil tagliatelle in a large pan of salted boiling water until 'al dente'.

Drain then rinse with hot water to remove excess starch.

Pre-heat oven to 190°C / gas mark 5.

Separate eggs and whip egg whites until stiff.

Add yolks, cheese and spring onions.

Season with pepper and salt.

Gently fold in beaten egg whites.

Put into shallow casserole and dot with butter.

Bake for approximately 30 minutes, until golden brown.

Serve with a mixed green salad.

Frühlingsnudeln – Spring Vegetable Pasta (V)

This is a wonderful way to make good use of really fresh vegetables. You can vary the vegetables and alter quantities to suit your taste. The important features are the variety, the slightly undercooked vegetables, and the combination of herb butter and thin noodles.

Ingredients

300g fresh vermicelli or very thin spaghetti
200g shelled peas
250g asparagus
250g shelled broad beans
2 tbs good olive oil
50g butter
10 basil leaves
2 cloves of garlic, crushed
salt and pepper
freshly grated parmesan

Method

Remove the thin white skin from the broad beans (a bore, but worth it).

Add them to the peas.

Snap tough ends off the asparagus and chop the rest diagonally into 2cm pieces.

Put asparagus into a pan of boiling water, boil for 30 seconds, drain.

Mix butter with garlic and chopped or torn basil leaves.

Boil pasta for approximately 5 minutes, depending on thickness. (Test to see if cooked.)

Heat the olive oil with garlic. Add the vegetables, and stew slowly for about 5 minutes.

Drain pasta, mix with vegetables and herb butter, season with freshly ground black pepper. Garnish with a few basil leaves.

Serve with grated parmesan.

Tip

*If you blanch the broad beans for a few minutes in boiling water,
the skins can be removed more easily.*

Salat – Salads

The word 'salad' instantly conjures up images of spring and summer in my mind. Indeed, there are few more tempting dishes than a well-presented salad of fresh English lettuce, tomatoes, and cucumber, preferably just picked from the garden, and accompanied by some cold meat, fish or cheese. In Central Europe, salads occupy a different place in the menu. They are mostly served with a vinaigrette dressing and frequently replace cooked vegetables as an accompaniment to a main meat or fish course.

Methods of cooking main courses vary substantially from country to country. A lot of British meals are served with gravy or sauce. Many meals on the Continent consist of crisply fried foods such as Schnitzel, fish or burgers, and these are often accompanied by just a potato dish and salad, taking the place of gravy. Meat dishes are often served with only a small amount of natural meat juices, and therefore require either a vegetable with some sauce, or a suitable salad.

Vinaigrette (V)

The classical French dressing consists of 2–3 parts olive oil to 1 part wine vinegar, sometimes with ½ tsp French mustard.

Many cooks create their own versions of vinaigrette. Austrians tend to dilute their vinaigrette, often adding a little sugar, and they rarely use olive oil, which they find too pungent. My own version, on which even my family is divided, is given here.

Ingredients

    125ml olive or corn oil
    125ml white wine vinegar
    125ml water
    1 tsp sugar
    ½ tsp French mustard
    occasionally I add 1 clove of garlic, crushed

Method

Put all ingredients into a jar with a tight fitting lid, and shake until emulsified.

I usually make enough for two or three salads, as the dressing keeps well for a few days.

Mayonnaise (V)

Making mayonnaise used to be thought of as a difficult task when only a wooden spoon and bowl were available. But it is not difficult – you just need a strong wrist, and patience to dribble the oil into the egg mixture at a very slow and gentle speed. It is rather fun to do, and during my teaching career I always started it off in this manner to 'break the taboo'. Nowadays, most people have a rotary whisk, or an electric mixer, which enables you to achieve a good mayonnaise in minutes. Even when things go wrong, and you end up with a mixture looking like scrambled eggs, you can retrieve it by starting afresh with another egg yolk, and dribbling the failed concoction into it gradually.

Ingredients

2 egg yolks (the freshest eggs only, at room temperature)
1 tsp dry mustard
1 tsp sugar
1 tsp salt
white pepper
3 tsp lemon juice or wine vinegar
275ml corn oil (or a mixture of olive oil and corn oil – olive oil alone is rather pungent)
1 tbs boiling water

Method

In a small-ish bowl (to get maximum friction) beat yolks until creamy. Add seasoning.

Add 1 tsp lemon juice and beat.

Pour oil into a suitable jug and dribble into mixture drop by drop, gently running it down the side of the bowl.

Once it thickens to the consistency of cream, oil can be added a little faster.

Intersperse adding oil with lemon juice.

Add hot water at the end to get desired consistency.

Mayonnaise made in a blender

Although it is easy to buy ready-made mayonnaise, here is a recipe which is simple to make and far superior in flavour. As there is no preservative in this version, the keeping quality is reduced, but it will nevertheless keep for up to 3 weeks in a fridge. Most people nowadays have a blender, and whilst this is not the classic method, I find it the most convenient and, just as importantly, infallible.

It is necessary to use the freshest eggs available, and remember that, since you are using uncooked eggs, there could be a very slight health risk for any vulnerable guests.

Ingredients

1 whole egg (or 2 egg yolks)
1 tsp dry mustard
1 tbs lemon juice
1 tsp sugar
½ tsp salt
pepper
125ml light olive oil
125ml corn or rapeseed oil

Method

Put the egg into blender goblet.

Add seasoning, mustard and sugar. Blend until emulsified.

Add lemon juice and whizz for a few seconds.

Open the lid and very slowly drizzle in the oil whilst continuing to blend until thick.

Finally, add a little boiling water to get the correct consistency.

Potato Salads (V)

Potato salad is very popular in my family. I make two versions. One is dressed with mayonnaise, the other with vinaigrette. The waxier the potatoes, the better. Small salad potatoes are available now and even the kidney-shaped ones can sometimes be purchased. Whichever potatoes are used, boil them unpeeled until just tender. Peel whilst warm, but allow to cool before slicing them as thinly as possible.

The man in my house likes the typical Austrian version, with slices of waxy potatoes floating in ample vinaigrette; the rest of the clan prefer the mayonnaise dressing. I can never make enough, and as the grandchildren have grown, so have my serving dishes.

Kartoffel Mayonnaise Salat – Potato Mayonnaise Salad (V)

Ingredients

500g waxy potatoes (new potatoes are excellent; avoid King Edwards)

1 medium onion, or spring onions, or both

2 or 3 pickled gherkins

4 tbs mayonnaise (or 2 tbs yoghurt and 2 tbs mayonnaise)

1 tbs vinegar from the gherkin jar

salt and pepper

chopped chives or parsley (for garnish)

Method

Wash and boil potatoes in their skins until just tender.

When cool enough to handle, peel, and leave to get cold.

Finely chop onion and slice gherkins thinly.

Mix mayonnaise (plus yoghurt, if using) with vinegar and seasoning.

Slice cool potatoes into thin rings.

Combine everything and adjust seasoning.

If more liquid is needed, add a little more dressing or vinegar.

Leave for at least 30 minutes to allow flavour to develop.

This salad keeps well in the fridge for several days.

Tip

Left-overs can be used for making Swedish Herring Salad (page 10).

Erdäpfelsalat –
Potato Salad the Austrian Way (V)

Ingredients

500g waxy potatoes
1 onion
1 cup of vinaigrette (page 114)
freshly ground black pepper
½ tsp salt

Method

Wash and boil potatoes in their skins until just tender.

When cool enough to handle, peel, and leave to get cold.

Chop onions finely.

Slice potatoes thinly when cold.

Add vinaigrette and onions to potatoes. Season to taste.

Tip

There is an abundance of liquid in proportion to potatoes in this recipe, which makes it an excellent accompaniment to certain dishes, for example Schnitzel (page 54) or fried fish.

Gurkensalat – Cucumber Salad (V)

Very popular in Austria, this is an absolute essential with Eiernockerln (see page 101), and is regularly served during the summer months as a side salad for all sorts of main courses. To be successful, it is essential to slice the cucumber as thinly as possible, using a mandolin or food processor. Incidentally, the German name for mandolin is 'Gurkenhacke', meaning cucumber slicer.

Ingredients

1 large cucumber
1 tsp salt for marinading
1 clove of garlic, crushed
freshly ground black pepper
a sprinkling of paprika or fresh dill
about 150ml vinaigrette (page 114)

Method

Peel and slice cucumber as thinly as possible.

Put into a bowl and sprinkle with salt. Press down with a saucer and leave for at least 1 hour. (This will extract a lot of water and is essential for a successful salad.)

Strain the cucumber in a sieve, and squeeze either with hands (my method) or with the back of a spoon. Most of the salt will be poured off.

Rub the garlic round the serving dish.

Put in the cucumber, vinaigrette, pepper, and paprika or dill (no more salt is needed).

Taste to adjust seasoning. (You may want a little more sugar etc.)

Tip 1

In Britain most cucumbers are hot-house grown and quite delicate, so it is often possible to leave the skin on, which is recommended nutritionally. In hotter climates cucumbers are grown outdoors, becoming larger and coarser. Occasionally these can be bitter at each end, and it is therefore advisable always to taste before slicing.

Tip 2

Gurkensalat is usually served with a vinaigrette, as in this recipe, but it is also excellent with sour cream or Greek yoghurt, and sprinkled with chopped fresh dill.

Karfiol und Karotten Salat –
Cauliflower and Carrot Salad (V)

This is a salad I used to eat at a coaching house hotel in Bolton, when I worked in the area as a social worker. It is a 16th-century building, and used to serve remarkably cheap buffet lunches. This was my treat when the going got tough at work.

Ingredients

1 small cauliflower
1 carrot
2 tbs mayonnaise
2 tbs yoghurt
1 tsp French mustard
½ tsp curry powder
seasoning to taste
chives or parsley

Method

Break up cauliflower into small florets and cook in salted water until barely tender.

Strain and arrange on a platter.

Coarsely grate carrot. Arrange it round the cauliflower.

Season with salt and pepper.

Drizzle with curry-flavoured mayonnaise.

Sprinkle with chopped chives or parsley.

Tip

Served with a jacket potato and/or garlic bread, this salad makes a good light lunch.

Karfiol und Paprika Salat – Cauliflower and Pepper Salad (V)

This is a variation on the previous recipe.

Ingredients

1 red and 1 green pepper, sliced
1 cauliflower
some olives
1 tbs capers
spring onions, chopped
1 clove garlic, crushed
½ medium cup of vinaigrette (page 114)
paprika for sprinkling

Method

Break up cauliflower into small florets and cook in salted water until barely tender.

Strain, cool, and mix with peppers, spring onions and capers.

Add the garlic to the vinaigrette.

Coat vegetables with vinaigrette, sprinkle with paprika, and garnish with olives.

Karottensalat – Carrot Salad (V)

We had this salad whilst staying at a kibbutz in Israel, some 30 years ago. There were vegetables in abundance, all grown there on the kibbutz. The workers had been working in the fields since 5.30am and at 9am they sat down to their second breakfast. It consisted of freshly picked tomatoes, peppers, cucumbers, cream cheese, and hard-boiled eggs – and this salad.

Ingredients

    3 medium carrots
    1 tbs sultanas
    1 tbs chopped walnuts
    1 small onion
    150ml lemon vinaigrette
    1 tsp honey or sugar

Method

    Wash and peel carrots, and grate on fine grater.
    Soak sultanas in boiling water for 10 minutes and strain.
    Chop walnuts coarsely.
    Chop onion.
    Add vinaigrette.
    Stir thoroughly and adjust seasoning to taste.

Tip

To make a lemon vinaigrette, use the recipe on page 114, replacing at least half of the wine vinegar with fresh lemon juice.

Fisolen-Paradeiser Salat – French Bean and Tomato Salad (V)

I got to know this salad some years ago on holiday in Krakow, when we were invited to the home of a distant cousin. It was a hot day, and we ceased to be tourists for a few hours. The tomatoes were rather different to English ones – much larger and fleshier – and the onions were very mild. Though I have tried, I have never been able to get exactly the same result. Was it perhaps holiday euphoria which distorted my perception? I have often since made this salad in summer, sometimes with just-picked produce brought by kind, green-fingered neighbours. It may not taste quite as it did in Krakow, but it is still very good.

Ingredients

    250g firm tomatoes
    250g French beans
    1 Spanish onion (or as mild as you can find)
    salt and pepper
    150ml vinaigrette
    chopped chives, or a few torn basil leaves (optional)

Method

Thinly slice tomatoes.

Remove strings from the beans and boil in salted water until just tender ('al dente').

Slice onion into thin rings.

Strain beans, rinse in cold water, then drain well.

Combine all ingredients. Add vinaigrette.

Season with freshly ground black pepper, salt, and a little honey for extra sweetness.

To turn this recipe into a main course Salade Niçoise, add the following:

Ingredients

1 small can of tuna fish
2 hard-boiled eggs
a few anchovy fillets (optional)
1 tbs black olives
1 clove crushed garlic
some crisp, shredded lettuce

Method

Mix the tuna and anchovies (if used) with the bean and tomato salad.

Arrange on a bed of shredded lettuce.

Decorate with slices or quarters of egg, interspersed with black olives.

Serve with garlic bread.

Gemischter Gemüse Salat – Coleslaw (V)

I tend to make this salad when I have been very busy or if I am a bit jaded and feel a boost is needed. Commercially produced coleslaw is readily available, but the proportion of mayonnaise to vegetables is far too high for both health and taste. Whilst I sometimes cheat and buy a small tub to add to my own ingredients (a handy tip), I am giving you the wholesome version, and you can experiment from there. A word of warning: whereas the commercial salad tends to keep for several days, the homemade kind is at its best when eaten on the same day. This is an ideal salad for entertaining, since it is easy to make in larger quantities.

Ingredients

½ or ¼ firm white cabbage (depending on size and quantity required)
2 carrots
1 stick celery
1 medium apple
1 small onion
1 dsp sultanas
1 dsp chopped walnuts (or salted peanuts – check for guests' allergies!)
1 tbs roasted pumpkin seeds (optional)

Dressing

1 tbs lemon juice
4 tbs mayonnaise (or half mayonnaise and half yoghurt)
salt and pepper
1 dsp honey

Method

Shred cabbage as finely as possible.

Grate carrots, and chop celery, onion and apple (the peel can be left on).

Mix dressing and combine all ingredients.

Adjust seasoning to get the right sweet/sour flavour.

Rote Rüben Salat — Beetroot Salad (V)

As mentioned previously, there are numerous Continental dishes where the traditional accompaniment is essential, and having one without the other is unimaginable. For example, this beetroot salad is a must with Jewish chopped fish, but it is also frequently served as a side salad for other dishes.

Ingredients

225g cooked beetroot
½ tsp grated horseradish (if available) or
1 tsp horseradish sauce (readily available)
1 turnip
salt and pepper
onion, finely chopped (optional)
150ml vinaigrette (page 114)

Method

Grate beetroot and turnip on coarse grater.

Grate horseradish on fine grater. (This will make you cry, but it is worth it!)

Mix everything together, add seasoning, and pour vinaigrette over.

Taste and add a little more sugar if necessary.

Bohnen Salat –
Butterbean (and Cress) Salad (V)

This is a salad one rarely comes across, yet it is nutritious, and adds variety to a buffet or family meal. It is a winter recipe, and stems from the time before an abundance of unseasonal vegetables were imported from all parts of the world, regardless of cost.

Ingredients

250g dried butter beans (or a 400g tin)
1 bunch of watercress if available (nice but not essential)
bunch of spring onions (or a small onion)
salt and pepper
vinaigrette (page 114)

Method

If using dried beans, soak overnight.

Strain liquid, cover with fresh water.

Add a small pinch of salt, boil until tender (only add a small amount of salt: too much tends to harden the beans).

Chop onions.

Mix cooked, strained beans with all the ingredients except watercress.

Season liberally.

Put beans into a serving dish and surround with watercress.

Tip

If watercress is not available, peppers and tomatoes make good alternatives.

Russischer Salat – Russian Salad (V)

A colourful winter salad which can be served as a main meal by adding either fish, hard-boiled eggs, cold chicken, or cold meats.

Ingredients

100g cooked beetroot
100g cooked potatoes
200g mixed frozen vegetables
2 pickled gherkins
½ red onion, finely chopped
3 tbs mayonnaise (or half mayonnaise and half yoghurt)

Garnish

hard-boiled eggs
seasoning to taste

Method

Cook frozen vegetables briefly.

Cut all other items into small cubes.

Mix all ingredients with mayonnaise.

Season to taste.

Serve this in the centre of a plate, surrounded by quarters of hard-boiled eggs.

Tip

For a bit of 'zing' you can add a little lemon juice.

Krautsalat – Cabbage Salad (V)

Although this salad is virtually unknown in Britain, it is a versatile salad, often served in Austria as a side dish to stews and casseroles as a substitute for pickled red cabbage. It is quite different from the popular coleslaw, which we have inherited from the USA.

Ingredients

½ firm white cabbage
approximately 225ml vinaigrette (page 114)
1 small onion
½ tsp caraway seeds
salt and pepper
sugar to taste
thinly sliced green pepper (optional)

Method

Shred cabbage very finely. (A mandolin or food processor will help.)

Put into a bowl and cover with boiling water.

Add a tsp of salt, then cover and leave for 30 minutes.

Strain cabbage and add caraway seeds. (The caraway is authentic, but optional.)

Add chopped onion and seasoning.

Add vinaigrette, toss well, and adjust seasoning to taste.

Tip

This salad is better if allowed to stand for a few hours. It will keep for several days in the fridge.

Mehlspeisen –
Puddings and Desserts

It is difficult to choose the recipes we like best. I find English puddings quite unique – particularly the steamed versions. Sticky Toffee Pudding, for example, which I always regard as a heart attack on a plate, is one which the man in my life finds irresistible. Shortcrust pastries, fruit pies and crumbles are well known, and recipes are usually handed down from mother to child. My children and grandchildren have all learnt to use pastry from a very early age. We hardly used plasticine for play, pastry being as much fun and more productive, if a little more messy.

So what to choose from my vast collection of recipes? I have not only inherited them from my mother and several aunts, but also collected them on my travels around the world. From dumplings and Strudels to Schwarzwaldtorte, from pancakes to Kaiserschmarren and Zabaglione – the choice seemed endless! So I decided to do what I have done throughout this book: include those recipes which are family and friends' favourites. As it happens, they tend to be the more economical dishes, both in expense and labour (with the odd exception). I always enjoy preparing these 'Mehlspeisen', and I hope that you, dear reader, will do so too.

Semmelschmarren –
Viennese Bread and Butter Pudding

The word Schmarren means something useless, or of no value. I do not know the origin of the word used in this sense, but I do know that there are a number of delicious desserts called Schmarren. They all have one thing in common: they are usually baked and served sprinkled with sugar and cinnamon, without any further decoration, cream or custard. The exception (there is always an exception) is the occasional addition of a plum or prune compote called Zwetschkenröster. Try to pronounce this word after a glass or two of wine!

I have served Semmelschmarren, a fusion of English bread and butter pudding and Austrian Schmarren, to visitors from Vienna, resulting in many requests for the recipe. It is equally popular with all my English friends, and is easy and cheap to make. So, what more can I say?

Ingredients
3 or 4 thick slices of white bread, crusts removed
margarine or butter to spread
1 apple
2 tbs sultanas
1 tbs sugar
¼ tsp cinnamon
1 egg
275ml milk
1 tbs sugar

Method
Pre-heat oven to 190°C / gas mark 5.
Butter a pudding basin liberally.
Butter bread and cut into 2cm strips.
Grate apple.
Mix cinnamon and sugar, and add raisins.
Lay a third of the bread on the bottom of basin.
Cover with half the grated apple and half the sugar mixture.
Put half the remaining bread on top.

Repeat, finishing with bread, buttered side up.

Beat together egg, milk and sugar. Pour on top of pudding.

Cover with clingfilm, putting saucer on top for a bit of weight.

Allow to stand for an hour (or can be left in fridge overnight).

Uncover, and bake for approximately 35 minutes until crisp and golden.

Serve with a further sprinkling of cinnamon and sugar.

Tip

Mix 1 dsp ground cinnamon with 250g sugar, and store in a jam jar. This is needed in many Continental recipes and is a good standby for baking.

Apfelstrudel — Apple Strudel

This is probably the best-known Austrian dessert and is available in many versions, deriving its name from its filling. The pastry is a type of pasta dough, and the Viennese housewife of my childhood prided herself on her ability to make this dough and stretch it as thin as tissue paper. It is then anointed with melted butter and filled with the fruit of the season, or sweetened cream cheese, or even savoury fillings such as spinach and / or cabbage.

On recent visits to Vienna, I have learnt that many women (and probably men!) now use commercial filo pastry, which gives good results, and is also described below. Though I also sometimes use bought filo pastry, I occasionally enjoy making the real thing. A breadmaker mixes a wonderful dough and takes care of the kneading. It is fun to get a lump of pliable dough and to pull it to the size of the kitchen table. It's a magic way to impress your children and grandchildren. You do need a good-sized kitchen table, a clean old tablecloth, some time, and patience. Skill is acquired over time: the more often you make it, the easier it becomes.

One of my family stories is that my grandmother, who made Strudels regularly for her large family, used to shout for my grandfather to come and assist her in rolling the filled strudel and transferring it to the baking tray. The poor man, who ran an off-licence, had to stop serving his customers when he got the command. My mother repeated this story whenever I watched her making Strudel.

There are festivals in Austrian villages where they have Strudel-making competitions. I believe it is the length of the Strudel that counts. (We are talking of metres in double figures!)

A Strudel can be made with a pastry or a yeast dough, can have various fillings, and if it is for domestic consumption rather than a competition contestant, it will be curved into the original horseshoe shape. A traditional Apfelstrudel recipe comes next. You will find recipes for yeast Strudels later in the book.

Ingredients

Dough

    175g strong white bread flour (contains more gluten than ordinary flour and makes for greater elasticity)
    1 dsp vegetable oil
    1 tsp vinegar
    1 egg
    approximately 80ml warm water
    pinch of salt

For brushing and basting:

    3 tbs melted butter (preferably unsalted)

Filling

    1kg cooking apples (peeled, cored, thinly sliced)
    50g sultanas
    25g walnuts, chopped
    50g sugar mixed with ½ tsp cinnamon
    3 tbs dried breadcrumbs, fried in 50g butter or oil until golden

Method

Pre-heat oven to 180°C / gas mark 4.

Sift flour and salt into a bowl.

Add oil, vinegar, egg and warm water.

Mix these to a dough, aiming for a pliable consistency.

Generously flour a pastry board or working surface.

Knead the dough until it is smooth and no longer sticky. (If you have a breadmaker, this can be done in the machine.)

Put the lump of dough on the edge of the board.

Bring a small pan of water to the boil on the stove.

Empty the water and immediately tip the hot pan over the paste.

Leave it to rest in the steam for about 30 minutes.

Spread the tablecloth over the table.

Sprinkle liberally with flour.

Put the dough into the centre.

Using a well-floured rolling pin, roll the dough out to about 20cm.

Rub your hands with oil, slide them under the dough, palms down, and pull gently, using your knuckles rather than fingertips. This helps to avoid tearing.

Work from the middle outwards. Once the middle is thin you can move along.

The shape is not important, just stretch it as far as you can.

Ignore the odd tear, it will be covered as you roll it.

Trim the outer edges off with a sharp knife.

The pastry should be thin enough for you to be able to read some written words underneath it – seriously!

Now brush the entire surface with melted butter.

Spread the half of the dough nearest to you with buttered breadcrumbs.

Cover this crumbed surface with apples, sultanas and sugar.

Starting with the side nearest to you, lift up the cloth and carefully roll the dough up, allowing gravity to assist you.

Dampen the edges and tuck in. Shape the roll into a crescent. (This will help to fit it onto the baking tray.)

Grease a deep baking tray and invert it onto the Strudel.

Tuck the tablecloth in around the tray, and flip it over.

It takes courage but it does work.

Brush Strudel with melted butter.

Bake for about 40 minutes, basting occasionally.

Remove when golden brown and crisp.

Cut into serving portions and sprinkle liberally with icing sugar.

Serve either warm or cold (equally good), but to be authentic you never serve it with cream.

Now the easy way to make Apple Strudel, using ready-made filo pastry...

Ingredients

8 sheets of filo pastry
4 tbs melted butter (or half butter half oil)
filling as for traditional Apfelstrudel (but ½ the quantity)
floured tea towel

Method

To get a larger size, join 2 sheets of filo pastry by wetting the overlapped edges.

Brush with butter.

Put 4 layers on top of each other, brushing each layer with butter.

Spread breadcrumbs along half of the pastry lengthwise.

Put filling on top.

Roll up, and manoeuvre the Strudel onto a greased baking tray.

Bake as for traditional Apfelstrudel.

Palatschinken – Pancakes

In Austria pancakes are not a special feature in the calendar as they are in England, but are eaten on many occasions, with a variety of sweet or savoury fillings. They are often filled with apricot jam, or Powidl (prune conserve, see page 244), or with a sweetened cream cheese filling, served with sour cream or Greek yoghurt. I have further extended the range by adding rum to squeezed lemon juice and experimenting with various kinds of Crêpes Suzette. And, when the batter or the frying pan do not behave themselves, you can always tear up the misshapen pancakes, add a few sultanas, sprinkle them with cinnamon sugar, and serve them as Kaiserschmarren (see recipe on page 164).

Ingredients for the basic batter *(Makes about 8 pancakes)*
100g self-raising flour
pinch of salt
1 egg
1 medium cup of milk
corn oil for frying

Method
Sift flour and salt.

Put into mixing bowl with egg and half the milk.

Beat well until smooth. (You could use a balloon whisk, electric beater or food processor.)

Add remainder of the milk, aiming for the consistency of thick cream.

More milk or water can be added if necessary. Leave to stand for 30 minutes.

Heat frying pan until hot. (This prevents the batter from sticking.)

Put about 1 tsp oil into frying pan. Swivel it around to get hot, then pour half a small ladle of batter in, and tip the pan until the batter covers the base.

Ensure that the pancake is thin.

Cook until mixture sets and lifts up easily from the sides.

Turn and cook on the other side.

Although pancakes are at their very best when eaten straight from the frying pan, it makes it impossible for the cook to enjoy them with the family. They can be made in a batch, and kept warm on a plate over a pan of steaming water, or quickly reheated, covered, in a microwave oven.

They freeze very well, and can be reheated as above.

Tip

These pancakes should be much thinner than their English cousins. It is said that if they are thick enough to toss, you can toss them out of the window!

Topfenpalatschinken (Blintzes) – Cream Cheese Pancakes

Ingredients

pancakes as in previous recipe, with the following filling:
250g cream cheese such as Quark, curd cheese, or
    sieved cottage cheese
1 egg yolk
grated zest of 1 lemon
1 dsp sugar
butter or oil for frying
250ml sour cream or Greek yoghurt for serving

Method

Mix all the filling ingredients.

Put 1 dsp cream cheese filling on each pancake.

Roll up, tucking in the sides.

Put them close together in a suitable dish. (This stops them from unrolling.)

Refrigerate. (Can be left overnight, covered.)

Melt butter in frying pan, and carefully fry each pancake roll until golden and crisp on both sides.

Eat as soon as possible, sprinkled with icing sugar and served with cold sour cream or yoghurt.

Tip

When entertaining, you can fry the pancakes in advance, refrigerate them, and reheat them in a hot oven for approximately 15 minutes.

Crêpes Suzette

For that special occasion!

Ingredients

  8 pancakes (page 140)
  75g butter (margarine will not do)
  75g icing sugar
  1 orange and 1 lemon
  1 tbs orange liqueur (Cointreau or similar)
  1 tbs brandy for flaming

Method

  Cream butter and sugar.

  Grate zest of lemon and orange. Squeeze juice, and add to above with orange liqueur.

  Spread filling onto each pancake, then fold into quarters.

  Put into frying pan. Fry until filling is melted, turning pancake in the juice.

  Pour brandy into the pan and flame (standing well back).

  Serve immediately, garnished with an orange twist.

Tip

Any pancakes left over can be cut into very thin strips (this is an Austrian soup garnish called Fridatten – see page 20), and added to clear beef or chicken soup.

Scotch Pancakes

I cannot omit the recipe for Scotch pancakes or drop scones. These are simple to make, are enjoyed by children and adults alike, and are a real treat for afternoon tea.

Ingredients

    2 cups of self-raising flour
    2 level tsp baking powder
    150ml milk
    1 egg
    1 dsp sugar
    1 dsp syrup (or sugar)
    a little oil for frying

Method

Mix the ingredients into a batter. It should be slightly thicker than pancake batter.

Brush a heavy frying pan or griddle with a little oil and heat.

Take 1 tbs of batter and drop the mixture from the point of the spoon.

As soon as bubbles appear, turn the pancakes over.

Once they are cooked, put them on a plate inside a folded tea towel. (This keeps them soft.)

Serve buttered, with jam.

Israeli Pancakes

I had these little pancakes on a holiday many years ago, and have made them frequently since, either for afternoon tea or as a dessert, serving them with jam, raspberry coulis, stewed fruits or fresh fruit.

Ingredients

225g cream cheese
2 eggs
pinch of salt
50g sugar
75g self-raising flour
oil for frying

Method

Beat eggs and sugar.

Add cream cheese. Beat.

Add sifted flour.

Fry tablespoonsful of mixture in a lightly greased frying pan.

Apfel im Schlafrock – Apple Fritters

The literal translation for this is 'Apple in a Dressing Gown'. My mother always used the simple pancake batter (see page 140) and, provided that the apples are good, the oil is fresh and the frying is done correctly, the result is excellent. As I became more interested in culinary skills, I experimented with different batters, such as using beer instead of milk, using more eggs, and beating egg whites. But perhaps it would be best if you try my mother's basic recipe, and experiment later.

Ingredients

    2 large cooking apples (Bramley, if available)
    pancake batter
    corn oil or any good vegetable oil for frying
    ½ tsp cinnamon
    2 tbs sugar

Method

    Peel and core apples, using apple corer or small knife.

    Cut into slices about 1cm thick.

    Heat oil in large frying pan until almost smoking.

    Have the pancake batter and apples ready.

    Dip apple rings into batter, and lower them into the hot fat.

    Turn heat to low to avoid the batter burning and the apples remaining hard.

    When the underneath turns golden, turn them and cook the other side.

    Remove onto kitchen paper to absorb excess fat.

    Sprinkle with cinnamon and sugar, and serve as soon as possible.

Kastanienreis – Chestnut Surprise

One of my vivid childhood memories is the cold winter days in Vienna, my hands aching and freezing, seeking out the chestnut sellers offering their wares from behind their braziers. They were making roasted chestnuts and jacket potatoes. The distinctive smell and the warmth emanating from the braziers still gives me a comfortable feeling. I preferred to spend my pocket money on these, rather than on sweets. The chestnuts came in a cone made of newspaper, as did the potatoes, which were drenched with salt (no known health hazard then).

Kastanienreis is a simple, easily made concoction of roasted chestnuts and cream, the only tedious task being the peeling of chestnuts. But then, you can buy your way out of that chore.

Ingredients

   500g chestnuts, or 275g vacuum-packed chestnuts,
      or 475g tin chestnuts
   125ml milk
   vanilla pod or ½ tsp vanilla essence
   275ml double or whipping cream
   2 tbs sugar

Method

   If using fresh chestnuts, slit them with a sharp knife, place on a baking tray, and put into a hot oven until the shells open. They should then peel easily.

   Put shelled chestnuts into a pan, and add milk, vanilla and 1 tbs sugar.

   Simmer gently until chestnuts are soft.

   Grate the chestnuts (they should look like rice). You can use a food processor, a potato ricer, or Mouli grinder, or possibly even a coarse sieve.

   Do not stir the sieved chestnuts; they should remain fluffy.

   Pile into suitable individual dishes.

   Whip cream until stiff, adding sugar gradually.

Pipe a generous amount of cream on top of the chestnuts.
Decorate with a little grated chocolate or a whole chestnut.
Serve chilled.

Tip

Chestnuts can be cooked in the microwave: 6 slit chestnuts for 1 minute on full power.

Marillenknödeln – Apricot Dumplings

No Austrian cookery book would be complete without recipes for an assortment of dumplings. You will also find dumplings in the savoury 'Pasta and Dumplings' section; they do play a big part in the average Austrian household. Apricot dumplings are by necessity a summer dish, and are often only preceded by soup to make a complete meal.

When I was a child there were no shortcuts, and making these dumplings for a large family was a time-consuming job. Nevertheless, they were made and eaten by the dozen. There were competitions as to how many dumplings one person could eat. I remember reaching 12, my father beating me by eating 14!

This type of pudding was very much part of our family's summer diet, no matter what the circumstances, as the following recollection illustrates. We had left Vienna in 1939 and briefly lived in Prague before coming to England. As immigrants we lived in rented rooms but, undeterred, my mother continued to cook our meals on a primus stove (forerunner of Calor gas cookers). She still produced wonderful meals under extraordinary circumstances, and even entertained. On one occasion she entered the room with a platter of perfect dumplings, glistening with buttered breadcrumbs. Sadly, she tripped on a rug, and all the dumplings were sent flying. We ended up eating in a restaurant.

I must add that apricots grown locally were smaller than those we get in England, which are usually imported from countries with hotter climates. Frozen dumplings are now available in all Austrian supermarkets, but I hope that they are also still often made at home.

There are three main types of dough: potato, choux pastry and cream cheese. I believe that the most popular are made with the potato dough described below.

I do admit to occasionally cutting corners by using ready-cooked potato flakes – a trick I'm happy to share with you.

Ingredients

Dough (Makes approximately 12 dumplings – depending on size of fruit)
   450g potatoes or 100g instant potato flakes or powder
   25g margarine
   approximately 100g of plain flour (do not use self-raising)
   1 tbs semolina
   1 egg
   pinch of salt

Filling
   450g fresh apricots
   1 sugar lump for each apricot

Coating
   100g dried breadcrumbs
   50g margarine or butter
   sugar to sprinkle on when serving
   extra flour for moulding dumplings

Method

Either: boil potatoes in their skin until soft, peel and grate in a food processor or a potato ricer (a gadget available in specialist shops)

Or: reconstitute 100g of instant mashed potato according to instructions, *but* only use half the amount of boiling water. Aim for a dry potato consistency.

Add margarine, egg, and flour.

Mix to a pliable dough. If too soft, add semolina until the right consistency is obtained. (Practice makes perfect.)

Remove stones from apricots, trying to do so without splitting them completely.

Replace each stone with one sugar lump.

Working on a board coated with flour, form dough into a 5cm-diameter sausage.

Cut 2–3cm slices. Pat them flat.

Put apricot into the centre and mould dough around it, ensuring that there are no gaps.

Flour your hands liberally to avoid the dough sticking to them.

Put the ready-shaped dumplings on an oiled plate.

Bring a large pan of water to the boil, adding 1 tsp salt.

When all the dumplings have been shaped, drop them gently into the boiling water.

Boil for approximately 15 minutes or until they float up to the surface.

Whilst they are boiling, heat butter in a large frying pan, add breadcrumbs and fry until golden.

When dumplings are ready, remove with slotted spoon.

Immediately put them into the pan with fried breadcrumbs.

Toss gently until they are all coated with the buttered crumbs.

Sprinkle liberally with sugar and serve as soon as possible.

These dumplings freeze well and can be reheated, either in the microwave (uncovered) or over steam.

Tip 1

If they need to be kept warm, put them, still in the frying pan,
over a pan of boiling water.

Tip 2

You can change the filling according to the season:
cherry dumplings in spring, apricots in summer and plums in autumn.

Cream Cheese Dough
(An easy alternative to potato dough)

Ingredients

250g Quark or cream cheese
125g plain flour
125g dried breadcrumbs
1 egg

Method

Work the above ingredients into a pliable dough.

Proceed as with potato dough (page 150).

Salzburger Nockerln – Salzburg Soufflés

This recipe was given to me by a friend who inherited it from her mother. It must be a century old. I feel privileged to have been given such a treasure. Not only is Salzburg famous for Mozart and its music festivals, but also for its food in general, and Salzburger Nockerln in particular.

These are not difficult to make but, like any soufflé, they need to be made to order and served immediately, which is a tall order for any restaurant chef – hence the exorbitant price usually charged.

In a restaurant, one portion is usually sufficient for two or three people, and as the original recipe contains 7 eggs, I was delighted to be given this recipe which uses more reasonable proportions.

Ingredients
70g butter
50g sugar
4 eggs, separated
3 tbs plain flour
1 tbs cornflour
1 tsp vanilla essence or a vanilla pod
275ml milk

Method
Pre-heat oven to 180°C / gas mark 6.

Put milk into an ovenproof baking dish (a deep Swiss roll tin, or roasting tin) with vanilla essence or pod. Bring to boil.

Whisk butter and half the sugar.

Add egg yolks, and sieved flours.

Beat egg whites until stiff, gently fold remaining sugar into the mixture. Gently combine all ingredients.

Drop large spoonfuls into the hot milk. (Try to keep them separate.)

Bake until golden, for about 10–12 minutes. The milk will have been absorbed.

Remove to a warm serving platter. Sprinkle with icing sugar and serve immediately.

Schokoladecreme – Chocolate Mousse

Chocolate mousse is one of the most popular desserts: it looks attractive served in tiny mocha cups, giving you the opportunity to show off the coffee set you may have hidden away in some cupboard.

You can soak the sponge fingers in the spirit of your choice, adding something special to the more 'ordinary' (and sometimes a little too dense) chocolate mousse. My preference is for a particular Austrian rum which is 80% vol., and a superb ingredient for all sorts of creams and sauces. Sadly, I don't think it is available in Britain, but that may be one of many good reasons to visit Austria.

Ingredients *(For 6 small cups)*

6 sponge fingers (or trifle sponges)
5 tbs rum (or alternative of your choice)
3 eggs, separated
1 tbs sugar
1 tsp instant coffee granules dissolved in 1 dsp hot water
125g dark chocolate (70% cocoa solids if possible)

Method

Put a sponge finger (whole or broken) at bottom of each cup.

Moisten with rum (or alternative).

Beat egg yolks with sugar.

Put chocolate into a large pudding basin.

Bring a pan of water to boil. Put pudding basin on top. Do not let the bottom of the basin touch the water. If chocolate overheats it becomes grainy, which spoils the texture.

When chocolate has melted, add egg yolks and coffee.

Beat egg whites until stiff. Gently fold into the cooled chocolate mixture.

Put this on top of the soaked sponge fingers.

Decorate as you wish (whipped cream, chopped nuts, grated chocolate etc.)

Tip

A word of warning: at 80% vol. this Austrian rum is not for drinking neat, but it is wonderful added to a cup of tea instead of milk. Add a little honey and lemon juice to this brew and you have a soothing drink for a sore throat!

Nussnudeln –
Tagliatelle with Ground Walnuts

To have pasta as a pudding may seem unusual, but it is popular in Austrian desserts. It is sometimes served with sweetened cream cheese, or with poppy seeds. This particular dish has always been a family favourite and is extremely easy to make.

Ingredients

175g tagliatelle
1 tbs butter
110g ground walnuts
110g sugar

Method

Cook tagliatelle in plenty of salted water, being careful not to overcook.

Grind walnuts in a food processor or mill, and mix with sugar.

Drain pasta and rinse with hot water.

Melt butter in a pan, toss drained pasta in the butter until coated.

Serve immediately on a hot platter, sprinkled with some of the nut mixture. Hand round the rest of the nuts so that everyone can help themselves.

Lokshenpudding – Baked Noodle Pudding

A Jewish speciality, this is a more elaborate version of the previous recipe, with the advantage that it can be prepared a few hours in advance and baked just before serving.

Ingredients

100g egg tagliatelle
1 egg
½ tsp cinnamon
2 tbs sugar
50g chopped walnuts
1 grated apple
25g margarine
1 tbs currants
1 dsp oil

Method

Pre-heat oven to 170°C / gas mark 3.

Cook tagliatelle in plenty of salted water, being careful not to overcook.

Drain and rinse in cold water.

Mix all the other ingredients together and stir into noodles.

Put the oil in a baking dish and heat for a few minutes in the oven.

Add the noodle mixture and bake for approximately 35 minutes.

Pudding should be crisp on top, but soft inside.

Sprinkle with icing sugar to serve.

Weinschaum – Chaudeau (akin to Zabaglione)

Although I have made this dessert many times, I have to admit that it has not always been 100% successful. It is made from simple ingredients which are readily available and, at its best, is wonderfully fluffy, with a unique taste. When not absolutely successful it will be a bit more liquid than it should be, but the taste will still be divine.

When my children were small, there were always some sponge fingers in the tin. Later their use was less frequent, but once grandchildren arrived, they became important again. Alas, they too have now outgrown that stage, but they happily tuck into the Weinschaum, which is served in wine glasses.

Ingredients

  8 sponge fingers
  2 egg yolks
  2 tbs water
  3 tbs Marsala or a medium sweet sherry
  1 tbs sugar

Method

  Choose a bowl that will fit into the top of a pan without touching the bottom.

  Wedge the basin into the top of the pan containing boiling water, so that the water simmers against the outside of the basin.

  Break 1 or 2 sponge fingers into each wine glass.

  Put a little extra wine in each glass.

  Put all the other ingredients into the bowl sitting on the pan, whisk until the mixture is the consistency of thick cream.

  Pour immediately onto the sponge fingers, and serve right away.

Schneenockerln – Floating Islands

This is a pudding which is easy to prepare, very light (no fat), can be made hours in advance, and can be garnished according to mood and/ or season.

Ingredients

3 or 4 medium eggs, separated (kept at room temperature)
½ litre milk
1 tsp vanilla essence or a vanilla pod
125g sugar
2 dsp sugar (for custard)
25g cornflour
grated chocolate
a large frying pan with a lid

Method

Heat the milk and vanilla essence in the frying pan.

Beat egg whites until stiff, gradually folding in 1 dsp sugar at a time.

When milk is just below boiling point, reduce heat.

Drop tablespoons of the meringue mixture into the milk. Try to keep them separate.

Simmer for 3 minutes, but do not let the milk boil.

Carefully turn the meringues, then simmer for a further 3 minutes.

With a slotted spoon, remove them and put them into a serving dish.

Measure milk in a jug: you will need 350ml.

Mix cornflour with 3 tbs cold milk.

Add egg yolks and sugar. Whisk and gradually add hot milk. Pour into pudding basin.

Put this into a pan of boiling water. The basin bottom must not touch the water. Stir constantly. When the custard thickens, pour it over cooked egg whites. They will float on top.

Refrigerate, and sprinkle with grated chocolate just before serving.

Tip

Egg whites kept at room temperature will give a bigger volume when beaten.

Soufflé Omelette

This is one of those dishes which can look and taste spectacular, only takes a few minutes to prepare, and uses ingredients most of us have in our fridges. It is fun to make and can be either sweet or savoury. I am including it in this section, with some suggestions for sweet fillings, but you could equally use savoury fillings such as cheese, sautéed mushrooms, or spinach purée (but omit the sugar).

Ingredients (For 1 large omelette, enough for 2 persons)

    2 eggs
    1 tbs cold water
    1 tsp sugar
    butter for frying, preferably unsalted (oil will do, but lacks flavour
        and colour)

Filling

    heated jam, or lemon curd, or rum and lemon juice, or raspberry
    coulis etc.

Method

    Separate eggs.

    Mix yolks with water.

    Whip whites until stiff, adding sugar whilst whisking.

    Stir yolks very gently into the stiff egg whites until combined, but
    still very fluffy.

    Dissolve 25g butter in frying pan until it starts to change colour.

    Pour in egg mixture.

    Leave on low heat until bubbles appear on top.

    Cover after first 2 minutes and cook for a further 2 minutes.

    To get a firmer texture, the omelette can be put under a hot grill
    for 1 or 2 minutes.

    Or: put in a hot oven (200°C / gas mark 6) for 10 minutes. For this
    you need an ovenproof frying pan.

    To fold, mark middle with spatula, add filling to one side, fold other
    side over.

    Flip onto a hot serving plate and sprinkle with icing sugar.

    Serve immediately.

Nusskipferln – Nut Crescents

Topfen Blätterteig – Cream Cheese Puff Pastry

This is an easy and excellent pastry which lends itself to any number of fillings, both sweet and savoury. You will find it in most bakeries and coffee houses, either called Kipferl (crescent) or Kolatschen (an envelope shaped pastry). It acquires the name of the filling, for example Nusskipferl (nut crescent) or Powidl Kolatschen (jam pocket).

Ingredients for the pastry *(Makes 18 crescents)*
   125g Quark or cream cheese
   125g butter (soft margarine will not do)
   125g plain flour with a pinch of salt

Ingredients for eggwash
   1 egg, beaten with 1 dsp of water

Method
   Pre-heat oven 225°C / gas mark 7.

   Sift flour and salt.

   Rub in butter. Work in cheese.

   Knead briefly on a floured board, wrap in clingfilm, then refrigerate whilst preparing the filling.

Ingredients for walnut or hazelnut filling

50g ground nuts
50g sugar
2 tbs milk
1 dsp currants

Method

Combine all ingredients to a paste-like consistency.

Roll pastry to the thickness of a £1 coin.

Using a plate as a guide, cut a 25cm circle.

Cut that into 8 portions (wedges), re-roll offcuts, and shape another portion.

Put 1 tsp of the nut mixture into middle of each wedge.

Roll up from the wide side, ending with the point on top.

Brush a little egg onto the point to make it stick.

Shape into a crescent.

Brush each crescent with egg wash.

Put on greased baking tray, and bake for approximately 20 minutes, until golden brown.

Cool on wire tray, and when cold sprinkle liberally with icing sugar.

Alternative fillings could be jam, Powidl (page 244), apple purée or sweet mincemeat.

Kaiserschmarren – Emperor's Frippery

This is a type of Viennese sweet 'Yorkshire pudding'. It is said to have been created through a culinary disaster produced by the Kaiser's chef. There are two versions: one is the baked version, and the other is made from a pancake batter. I give both versions here.

Kaiserschmarren is always served with stewed prunes or plums, or with a raspberry coulis, and finished off with a sprinkling of cinnamon sugar.

Ingredients

150ml milk
75g self-raising flour
2 eggs, separated
1 tbs sultanas
1 tbs sugar
50g butter, or 1 tbs corn oil
pinch of salt

Method

Pre-heat oven to 180°C / gas mark 4.

Sift flour into mixing bowl. Add salt.

Beat egg whites until stiff. Add sugar.

Add egg yolks and milk to flour and beat well.

Gently fold in beaten egg whites.

Add sultanas.

Melt butter in a metal baking tray (Swiss roll tin or similar).

When really hot, pour in batter.

Bake for approximately 30 minutes until golden.

Now take two forks, and pull it all apart into small pieces.

Return to oven for a further 5 minutes to crisp a little more.

Serve on a warm platter, with a sprinkling of icing sugar.

Easy version of Kaiserschmarren

Ingredients

cooked pancakes (page 140)
1 tbs butter and 1 tbs corn oil for frying
1 tbs raisins or sultanas
1 tbs sugar mixed with ½ tsp cinnamon

Method

Tear or cut up the pancakes.

Melt butter and oil in frying pan.

Add pancake bits and dried fruit, and toss until heated.

Serve with cinnamon and sugar.

Tip

An excellent way to use less than perfect pancakes.

Germknödeln — Boiled Yeast Dumplings

A speciality which is regarded as a big treat by many Austrians, Germknödeln are often available in mountain huts (those irresistible little Beisls – pubs – you sometimes reach after a long climb) and sometimes served at lunchtime as a *Speciality of the House*. They are rather large, very filling, and are frequently half of a two-course meal such as soup and Knödeln.

I hesitated to include them amongst my favourite recipes as opinions in my family are divided: daughter hates them; English son-in-law adores them, and it was his request to include them. How can I refuse?

Yes, they are a little stodgy, they do not look very impressive (but no boiled dumplings do), they are not always 100% successful and, worst of all, one has to boil them just before serving. Perhaps I'm not selling them very well, but the compensation is that they *do* always taste good!

Ingredients
½ quantity of yeast dough after the first stage of proving (see page 187)

Filling
Powidl (prune jam with a unique, pleasantly sour flavour. Obtainable only at a good delicatessen or Polish shop. You could make it yourself – see page 244 – or use apricot or damson jam as substitutes).

Topping
50g melted butter
1 tbs ground poppy seeds (use your coffee grinder) mixed with 3 tbs sugar
(ground walnuts can be used instead of poppy seed)

Method

Gently knead dough, roll into 7cm-diameter sausage.

Cut this into 8 portions, working on a well-floured board.

Press these portions into flat circles about 10cm in diameter.

Put a teaspoon of Powidl or jam into the middle of each circle.

Gather all the edges (like a little purse) and firmly squeeze together.

Put on a well-floured tray, cover with a tea towel and allow to prove in a warm place until well risen.

A large, wide pan is needed for boiling.

Fill it with water, bring to the boil, and let it simmer gently, adding 1 tsp salt.

With the help of a spatula lift 1 dumpling at a time, and put it into the boiling water.

Do not overcrowd the pan.

Boil gently for 3 minutes.

With a slotted spoon, turn over and continue to simmer for 4 minutes.

Melt butter in a large frying pan.

Lift Germknödeln out of the pan and immediately pierce them with a fork to let steam escape (this avoids them collapsing).

Put them into the melted butter, and serve as soon as possible with a liberal sprinkling of either poppy seed and sugar or nuts and sugar.

Tip

Germknödeln can be kept warm for a short while, either steamed over a pan of boiling water or in the oven with the door ajar.

The Ultimate English Trifle

I am indulging in adding this very English dessert to the book, mainly for my family: it is my daughter-in-law's favourite. Although there are endless recipes available, I was told by a very remarkable cookery teacher during the first stages of my professional training that this is the ultimate old English recipe. Note: there is no jelly, and even the fruit is optional.

Ingredients

1 Swiss roll filled with jam
75ml sherry
fresh or frozen raspberries
¼ litre milk
2 eggs
75g sugar
1 tsp cornflour
½ tsp vanilla essence
250ml double or whipping cream
1 tsp sugar

Method

Cut Swiss roll into slices and use to line a suitable glass dish.

Sprinkle sherry on the sponge.

Add raspberries, leaving some for decoration.

Bring milk to the boil.

Mix eggs, cornflour and sugar in separate basin. Add hot milk, stir well then return to low heat.

Simmer, stirring continuously, but avoid letting the mixture boil.

Add vanilla essence. Stir well, then pour over sponge.

Cover and refrigerate.

When cold, whip cream (if using double cream, add 1 dsp milk).

Add 1 tsp sugar just as the cream thickens.

Spoon or pipe this on top of the trifle.

Decorate with raspberries, and a little grated chocolate.

Torten, Kuchen und kleine Bäckereien – Gâteaux, Cakes and Biscuits

There is a connection between Austria's age-old coffee-house culture and the emergence of a vast selection of artistically displayed luscious cakes, Torten, and pastries, many of them sinfully oozing with whipped cream.

These are the coffee houses where, at the beginning of the 20th century, life-changing ideas in medicine, psychiatry, literature, philosophy, music, and politics were discussed. Inevitably this has declined in the last 60 years. Some of these famous coffee houses still exist, such as Sacher, Demel, Aida, and the famous Zauner in Bad Ischl. My childhood experience of these wonderful cakes came from my mother's kitchen, and from the occasional Sunday outing to a Konditorei (a bakery or patisserie), which was like an Aladdin's cave.

All the following recipes have been tried, tested and tasted over decades, and have my family's approval. I have adapted some of them to more reasonable quantities, and to fit in with current nutritional ideas.

Bischofsbrot – Bishop's Bread

I do not know how this fruit cake (it is not really a bread) acquired its name, but it is economical to make and has excellent keeping qualities, making a little bit go a long way. Perhaps it was cooked in monasteries in days gone by.

A great cake to make, it is fatless, therefore ideal for a low-fat diet. I have made this cake for my children and grandchildren, and it has been sent to Israel (where my son spent his gap year), and to East Africa (where his son spent his), and it always arrived intact. The recipe was given to me by an aunt who was known for her frugality; it suited her character! It keeps for a long time without going stale and can be cut into very thin slices. On top of all that, it actually tastes delicious.

Ingredients

3 eggs, beaten
100g caster sugar
150g mixed dried fruit
100g whole hazelnuts
150g self-raising flour
25g chocolate (chopped)
grated zest of 1 lemon

Method

Pre-heat oven to 180°C / gas mark 4.

Grease an oblong cake tin (approximately 10cm x 25cm).

Line tin with greaseproof paper, brush with oil.

Beat eggs, sugar and lemon rind until smooth and pale.

Sift flour, adding a pinch of salt.

Gently fold flour into the egg mixture.

Add dried fruit, whole nuts and chopped chocolate.

Pour into greased, lined tin.

Bake for approximately 40 minutes, until firm and a skewer inserted in the middle comes out clean.

Turn out onto cooling tray. When cold wrap in tinfoil.

Leave at least a day before cutting. Slices should be about 3mm thick.

Dundee Cake

No translation is needed for this favourite cake of one of my granddaughters. She took one back to university after each break. This is a very different recipe to Bischofsbrot: moist and rich, it should be cut into generous slices. It also improves if kept for a day or so before cutting, and will keep for a number of days in a cake tin. It freezes superbly.

The recipe was given to me by a Scottish lady who attended one of my 'International Cookery Classes', in exchange for the Bischofsbrot recipe. This exchange of ethnic food recipes was always a delight during my teaching career.

Ingredients

125g self-raising flour
120g butter or soft margarine
110g sugar
2 eggs
200g mixed dried fruit or
   75g stoned raisins
   50g sultanas
   50g currants
   25g mixed peel
25g glacé cherries
25g ground almonds
grated rind and juice of 1 lemon
1 tbs milk
25g whole blanched almonds

Method

Pre-heat oven to 180°C / gas mark 4.

Grease and line a deep 15cm tin (for a 20cm tin, double the quantities).

Wash and dry fruit.

Cream butter and sugar until nearly white.

Sift dry ingredients together.

Add beaten eggs and lemon juice, interspersed with a little flour.

Add lemon zest.

Add flour and ground almonds.

Finally, stir in fruit.

Fill cake tin, level the mixture.

Arrange blanched almonds on top of cake.

Bake for approximately 1 hour 15 minutes, or until a knife comes out clean. If sticky, bake for a further 10 minutes.

Leave for 10 minutes, then turn out onto cooling tray.

Apfelnusstorte – Apple-Nut Cake

This is an alternative to the English apple pie (which takes a lot of beating), and according to my youngest grandson, it is unsurpassable. The pastry is more of a shortbread, and the combination of fruit, spices and nuts makes for a delightful pudding, though it is equally good served cold as a Torte. Due to the high content of fruit and richness of pastry, it does not need any other embellishment such as custard or cream.

Ingredients

200g self-raising flour
175g butter
100g caster sugar
1 egg yolk
25g melted butter to brush on top

Filling

500g Bramley apples
25g chopped walnuts
50g sugar, mixed with ½ tsp cinnamon
1 dsp currants

Method

Pre-heat oven to 200°C / gas mark 6.

Grease a 20cm loose-based, deep cake tin.

Sift flour, adding a pinch of salt.

Rub in butter.

Add sugar and egg yolk.

Quickly combine above ingredients. (This can be done in a mixer, but do not overbeat.)

Wrap pastry in clingfilm. Refrigerate whilst you prepare the filling.

Peel and core apples. Slice thinly.

Mix with currants, nuts, sugar, and spice.

Take pastry from fridge. Reserve a small portion and divide the rest in half.

Roll one half to fit into cake tin.

From reserved portion make a 1cm sausage to fit round the base. Press this about 1cm up the sides of the tin.

Put filling into pastry base.

Roll second piece of pastry.

Draping it over the rolling pin, carefully place it on top of the filling.

Brush with melted butter.

Bake for approximately 35 minutes until golden brown.

Tip

When making pastry, try to keep hands as cool as possible (if necessary, rinse with cold water), rub in quickly with fingertips only, lifting the mixture to aerate it. The quicker you can do that, the better. This is particularly important when using soft margarine. Hardened margarine used to be recommended, but is now generally considered best avoided for health reasons.

Apfelkuchen – Danish Apple Cake

One of the quickest and most successful cakes in my repertoire is this recipe, given to me by one of my Danish friends. The fruit can be altered according to taste and season.

Ingredients
225g self-raising flour
1 egg
100g butter or margarine
50g sugar

Filling
500g cooking apples, peeled, cored, and thinly sliced
2 dsp brown sugar mixed with ½ tsp cinnamon
25g chopped walnuts
50g sultanas

Method
Pre-heat oven to 180°C / gas mark 4.

Grease a 23cm metal flan tin or loose based cake tin.

Sift flour into mixing bowl.

In a pan, melt butter without overheating – it just needs to be liquid.

Add butter, egg and all other ingredients to the flour.

Mix with a spoon.

Divide mixture in two and press one half into the bottom of the flan tin.

Top with apples and other ingredients.

Roughly scatter lumps of the remaining dough over the apples.

Bake for approximately 45 minutes.

Serve hot or cold. If cold it can be served plain, decorated with whipped cream, or served with ice cream.

Tip

When pressing the dough into the tin, use the knuckles of your hand.

Honigkuchen (Lekach) – Honeycake

A cake popular all the year round, but traditionally made for the Jewish New Year, the honey symbolises the hope for a 'sweet new year'. It is an interesting recipe, using oil instead of the more usual butter or margarine. The quantities for this cake are rather large, but since it keeps really well in a tin (or in the freezer) it is worth making a little bit extra. I make it in a large square tin and, when cold, cut it into several 10cm x 20cm strips, either to freeze or to give to friends and family to wish them a Happy New Year.

Ingredients

    450g self-raising flour
    175g sugar
    1 tsp mixed spice
    1 tsp cinnamon
    1 tsp ginger
    1 tsp bicarbonate of soda
    3 eggs
    1 medium cup corn oil or vegetable oil
    1 medium cup honey or syrup
    1 medium cup boiling water
    50g flaked almonds
    50g candied peel (optional)

Method

    Pre-heat oven to 170°C / gas mark 3.
    Grease a 25cm square, deep tin (or 2 smaller ones), and line.
    Sift all dry ingredients into a large mixing bowl.
    Beat eggs, add oil.
    Mix honey with boiling water.
    Add eggs and oil to honey and water.
    Add all dry ingredients.
    Mix everything together, stirring thoroughly.
    Add candied peel, if used.
    Pour mixture into the prepared tin.

Sprinkle with almonds.

Bake for approximately 1 hour.

Cool in tin for 15 minutes before turning out onto cooling tray.

Leave for 1–2 days before cutting, for flavour to develop, and for ease of cutting.

Tip

When using honey or syrup, dip spoon into flour before putting it into the honey – it will be easier to handle.

Obstkuchen – Fresh Fruit Cake

An ideal recipe to celebrate the fruit of the season, as it can be made with cherries, apricots or plums, the cake taking the name of the fruit:

- Kirschenkuchen – Cherry Cake

- Marillenkuchen – Apricot Cake

- Zwetschkenkuchen – Plum Cake

This cake can be made in an ordinary sandwich cake tin, or a flan tin, or if made in an oblong tin, it can be cut into slices or squares according to taste.

My parents seemed to find it necessary always to provide us with the first fruits of the season, when they were still scarce and expensive. The cake made a small quantity of fruit go a long way and was always a special treat. This was in the days before importation made summer fruits available all the year round (even if under-ripe and often tasteless).

Ingredients

175g self-raising flour
100g caster sugar
100g butter or soft margarine
2 eggs, beaten
grated zest and juice of 1 lemon
200g fruit of the season (apricots or plums are halved, stones removed)

Method

Pre-heat oven to 190°C / gas mark 5.

Liberally grease a 20cm round shallow cake tin, or oblong Swiss roll tin.

Cream butter and sugar until fluffy.

Sift flour.

Add beaten eggs to butter and sugar mixture gradually, with a little flour.

Carefully fold in sifted flour and grated lemon zest.

Consistency should be fairly stiff, but drop easily off the spoon.

If mixture is too stiff, add 1 tbs milk.

Spread mixture into the prepared tin.

Arrange fruit on top (apricots and plums with the hollow side up).

Bake in pre-heated oven for approximately 35 minutes.

Carefully remove onto cooling tray.

If baked in an oblong tin, cut into squares or slices while still in tin, and then remove to the cooling tray.

When cold, and just before serving, sprinkle liberally with vanilla-flavoured icing sugar.

Tip 1

*It is important to put the stoned fruit skin down onto the dough,
to avoid the sponge becoming soggy.*

Tip 2

*You can keep a jar of icing sugar with a vanilla pod in it,
ready to sprinkle whenever you need it.*

Ribiselkuchen — Redcurrant Meringue Slices

Redcurrants are much more popular in Austria than in England, whilst blackcurrants are hardly known there. This is an interesting recipe, mixing a tart fruit with the sweetness of the meringue.

Ingredients

225g shortcrust pastry made with:
    200g self-raising flour (or half self-raising and half plain)
    100g butter or soft margarine
    approximately 8 tsp cold water
    1 egg yolk
    2 tsp icing sugar dissolved in the egg yolk (optional)

Filling

250g redcurrants (stripped)

Topping

2 egg whites
100g sugar, plus 1 dsp to sprinkle on top

Method

Pre-heat oven to 200°C / gas mark 6.

Sift flour.

Rub butter into flour until crumbly.

Add water and egg yolk (with sugar, if used).

Knead quickly into dough.

Roll dough and line a shallow oblong baking tray.

Prick all over with fork.

Put into the freezer for 30 minutes.

Bake blind (without redcurrant filling) for 20 minutes.

Remove from oven and turn oven temperature down to 140°C / gas mark 1.

Cover thickly with redcurrants.

For the topping, whisk egg whites until stiff.

Add sugar gradually.

Whisk until mixture holds its shape if lifted with a spoon.

Spread this over the redcurrants then sprinkle with a little sugar.

Bake at the low temperature until crisp and set (approximately 1 hour).

Allow to cool, and cut into slices. Serve as soon as possible – meringues tend to loose their crispness after a while.

Tip 1

When using soft margarine, slightly less liquid is needed due to the consistency of the margarine.

Tip 2

Putting the empty pastry case into the freezer for a short while (it can also be cooked from frozen) will stop the mixture bubbling up when baked. Any left-over pastry can be used for jam tarts, pastry strudels etc.

Date and Walnut Cake

This is a popular English recipe. I produce large quantities of this cake at my annual Macmillan Coffee Mornings, along with various other tasty bakes. A little effort goes a long way.

Ingredients

200g self-raising flour
100g soft margarine
100g soft brown sugar
2 eggs
1 tsp vanilla essence
150ml boiling water
1 level tsp bicarbonate of soda
225g chopped dates
50g chopped walnuts

Method

Pre-heat oven to 180°C / gas mark 4.

Grease and line a loaf tin, 10cm x 20cm.

Chop dates, pour boiling water over them.

Cream margarine and sugar.

Add eggs and vanilla.

Add sifted flour.

Add dates and walnuts. Stir well to combine.

Pour into loaf tin and bake for approximately 40 minutes.

Test with skewer to see if ready. If skewer is sticky, bake a little longer.

Leave to cool for 10 minutes. Turn out onto cooling tray.

Leave for 24 hours before cutting into slices.

Zitronenkuchen – Lemon Drizzle Cake

I doubt if this cake is known in Austria. It is one of my grandson's favourite cakes and he baked it for himself from about the age of 10, just needing a bit of help initially with the hot oven and syrup. Now a couple of years older, he cooks it independently and is insulted if he is offered help. This is one of the useful, quick recipes where all the ingredients (except the syrup) are put into a bowl and beaten in one stage.

Ingredients

Cake

100g soft margarine
175g self-raising flour
175g caster sugar
2 lemons, zest finely grated, juice reserved for syrup
2 eggs

Syrup

75g sugar
juice of 2 lemons

Method

Pre-heat oven to 180°C / gas mark 4.

Grease a loaf tin, 10cm x 20cm, and line the bottom with a strip of greaseproof paper.

Beat margarine, flour, sugar, lemon zest, and eggs until smooth.

Put the mixture into prepared loaf tin and bake for approximately 40 minutes.

When finished, *do not* turn out.

Bring lemon juice and sugar to boil. Simmer until the mixture thickens slightly. Watch it – it must not caramelise.

Prick cake all over with a skewer and pour syrup over it.

Leave in tin until cake is cold.

———————

Tip

———————

Strictly for adult tastes only: try adding a dessertspoon of rum to the lemon syrup.

Lustkuchen – Passion Cake

Another name for this is Carrot Cake, adored by many (in the mistaken belief that it is a health food), but hated by my husband and son who insist that carrots have no place in a cake, but should sit next to a piece of meat or fish. It is usually finished with a delicious icing, and for special occasions can be decorated with little home-made marzipan carrots. My granddaughter had great fun as a young teenager producing one of these cakes for her mother's birthday.

Ingredients

250g self-raising flour
½ tsp bicarbonate of soda
1 tsp baking powder
1 tsp cinnamon
pinch of salt
200ml corn oil
250g soft brown sugar
3 eggs, separated
150g finely grated carrots
150g chopped walnuts
grated zest and juice of 1 orange

Frosting

200g soft full-cream cheese
75g icing sugar
2 tbs orange juice (or lemon juice)

Method

Pre-heat oven to 180°C / gas mark 4.

Grease and line 25cm cake tin.

Beat oil and sugar briefly.

Add yolks, orange zest, grated carrots, and chopped walnuts to oil and sugar mixture.

Sift together flour, bicarbonate of soda, baking powder, and cinnamon.

Fold into mixture.

Beat egg whites and fold in gently.

Pour into prepared tin and bake for approximately 45 minutes until cooked.

Remove from oven, leave in tin for 10 minutes before turning out onto cooling tray.

When cold, cover with frosting.

To make frosting

Beat cream cheese and sugar.

Add orange juice gradually.

Spread over the cooled cake.

Decorate with whole walnuts.

Tip

You can make little marzipan carrots with ready-made marzipan and orange and green food colourings.

Yeast Baking

For successful yeast baking it is vital to remember three important facts:

1. Heat kills yeast. Therefore any liquid added must be only warm (i.e. bath water temperature).

2. The dough and then the shaped items must each rise to approximately twice their original size. The time needed depends on the room temperature.

3. Whilst rising, keep dough covered either with oiled clingfilm or with a tea towel, and put in a warm – but not hot – place to rise.

Basic Yeast Dough

(Makes 1 medium-sized Guglhupf and 12 Schnecken, i.e. Viennese yeast buns, akin to Chelsea buns)

Ingredients

500g strong white flour
½ tsp salt
100g sugar
100g butter, margarine or corn oil
2 eggs
25g fresh yeast or 1½ tsp dried yeast
approximately 320ml warm milk (different flour brands absorb
   varying amounts of liquid)
grated zest of 1 lemon

Method

Sift flour into a large mixing bowl.

Melt butter.

Heat milk to lukewarm.

Put yeast into a cup. Add ½ cup of warm milk, allowing yeast to dissolve until it bubbles.

Make a well in the flour. Add eggs, milk, dissolved yeast, and lemon zest.

Mix with wooden spoon until it becomes a manageable dough.

Aim for a soft, pliable texture. (You can add more warm liquid, or more flour as necessary.)

Turn dough onto a floured board and knead until it becomes smooth and glossy.

(If you have a breadmaker or a large mixer, all the above can be done in the machine, following the manufacturer's instructions.)

Put the dough into a large, greased bowl to prove, covering with clingfilm or clean tea towel.

Leave in a warm, draught-free place until doubled in size.

Turn the risen dough onto a floured board, this time kneading it gently for about 2 minutes. It is now ready to be used in any of the following recipes.

Germguglhupf – Yeast Guglhupf

There is no literal translation for this cake, which is almost like a fruited teacake. The version made without yeast (see page 198) is similar to a marbled Madeira cake. What makes this special is the cake mould, which is a fluted tin with a funnel-shaped hole in the middle. This ensures an evenly golden finish when baked. You may be able to buy one of these tins in a speciality kitchen shop; if not, a trip to Austria may well be worth it!

Ingredients

half the given quantity of yeast dough (page 187)
2 tbs sultanas or mixed dried fruit
1 tbs skinned almonds or almond flakes

Method

Pre-heat oven to 190°C / gas mark 5.

Grease a medium-sized Guglhupf tin (an oblong cake tin would do, but you lose the distinctive shape) with butter, and sprinkle with dry breadcrumbs or flour.

When kneading the dough after the initial proving, work the dried fruit into the mixture.

Put almonds into the grooves of the Guglhupf tin or at the bottom of the cake tin.

Gently roll the dough into a thick sausage and place into the tin, patting it down.

Cover the tin with clingfilm and allow to rise until doubled in size. Remove clingfilm.

Put into oven and bake for approximately 30 minutes.

Test with skewer to see if cooked through (skewer should come out clean).

Turn out onto cooling tray.

When cold, sprinkle liberally with vanilla-flavoured icing sugar.

Tip 1

Keep a vanilla pod in a jam jar filled with icing sugar for a permanent supply.

Tip 2

To skin almonds, cover with water, bring to boil, strain. The skin then comes off easily.

Schnecken – Viennese Pastries

These look similar to Danish pastries, but contain much less butter and have a different texture. They can be made into a very attractive cake, or into individual buns of various sizes. They can be left plain, sprinkled with icing sugar, or glazed with a sugar glaze when taken out of the oven. The name Schnecken (which means snails) simply describes the shape of the finished buns.

All my family like them and I have had special requests for their inclusion here. Like all other yeast baking, they freeze really well for up to 2 months, provided they are well wrapped in clingfilm.

Ingredients
half the given quantity of dough on page 187
(makes 12 Schnecken)

Filling
1 tbs soft butter or margarine
2 tbs sugar mixed with ½ tsp cinnamon
2 tbs currants
1 tbs chopped walnuts

Sugar glaze (optional)
2 tbs icing sugar mixed with 1 tsp boiling water

Method
Pre-heat oven to 200°C / gas mark 6 and grease a baking tray.

After having re-kneaded the proved dough, roll it into an oblong about 15cm x 25cm.

Spread with softened butter.

Sprinkle with cinnamon and sugar.

Top with currants and walnuts.

Fold into a tight roll. Cut into 12 portions, placing them onto the baking tray with cut side up, leaving some space between them.

Cover with clingfilm and leave to rise until doubled in size.

Remove clingfilm.

Bake for approximately 30 minutes until golden brown.

Remove and cool on cooling tray.

If you want to glaze them, mix icing sugar with water and brush glaze over pastries as soon as they come out of the oven.

To shape them into a cake

Grease a 20cm shallow loose-bottomed flan tin with butter.

Put portions of filled dough all around nearly touching.

Fill the centre with remaining portions, then prove and bake.

When baked, slip them from the tin onto the cooling tray and glaze as above.

Nussstrudel — Walnut Roll

When we got married shortly after the end of the Second World War, most foods were still in short supply, and money was even scarcer. After our modest Register Office wedding in Oldham, my parents entertained all the guests at home with a huge array of yeast-baked specialities. It is a wonderful memory, more exceptional than if it had been a reception at the Dorchester! The marriage has lasted over 60 years despite its humble beginnings, and I have never stopped making yeast cakes.

The versatility of the yeast dough is endless, and it lends itself to almost any filling. Two good ones, walnut and cream cheese, are given here.

Ingredients
half given quantity of risen yeast dough (see page 187)

Filling
100g walnuts
25g breadcrumbs
2 tbs sugar
1 tbs currants
2 tbs milk

Method
Grind walnuts.
Add all other ingredients.
Add milk to get spreadable consistency.
Put dough on a floured board.
Pull or roll into an oblong, 20cm x 30cm.
Spread nut mixture onto dough, roll up (like a Swiss roll).
Transfer to greased baking tray.
Bake at 200°C / gas mark 6 for approximately 30 minutes.
Cool on a wire tray.
When cold, sprinkle with icing sugar and cut into 1cm slices.

Topfenstrudel – Cream Cheese Roll

Ingredients

half given quantity of risen yeast dough (see page 187)

Filling

225g Quark or cream cheese
grated zest of 1 lemon
1 egg yolk
1 tbs sugar
1 tbs sultanas

Method

Pre-heat oven to 200°C / gas mark 6, and grease a baking tray.

Put all filling ingredients in a bowl.

Mix to a spreadable consistency.

Put dough on a floured board.

Pull or roll into an oblong 20cm x 30cm.

Spread filling onto dough and roll up (like a Swiss roll).

Transfer to baking tray and bake for approximately 30 minutes.

Cool on wire tray.

When cold, sprinkle with icing sugar and cut into 1cm slices.

Kümmelbrot – Wholemeal Seeded Bread

Baking bread is therapy for me. I love the process of kneading the warm dough, the warmth of the oven and the aroma of baking. There is nothing to equal the satisfaction one gets in seeing the large, well-risen, shiny loaf emerge from the oven.

One of the things I have missed after moving from Manchester is the availability of really good bread from the numerous Jewish bakeries in that area. We do have some good bakeries where we live at present, but not even the best can match the ones I remember.

So I experimented and failed miserably with natural sourdough, but I have found a compromise which we all like and which I bake weekly. I do admit to being the owner of a breadmaker, and I do use it to knead and partly prove the dough, but then I shape it by hand and bake it in the oven.

Ingredients

   325g wholemeal bread flour (or 250g wholemeal and 75g rye)
   125g strong white bread flour
   2 tsp sugar
   2 tsp salt
   1 tsp dried yeast (or 15g fresh yeast)
   2 tbs caraway seeds (Kümmel, in German)
   1 tbs mixed seeds (rape, pumpkin, sesame)
   1 tbs oil
   approximately 300ml warm water

Method by hand

   Pre-heat the oven to 220°C / gas mark 7 and grease a baking tray.
   Dissolve yeast in 125ml warm water until bubbles appear.
   Put all dry ingredients into a large mixing bowl.
   Pour dissolved yeast into the centre.
   Add remainder of water, which should be warm but not too hot.
   Mix with spoon until well combined.

Turn onto floured board and knead until smooth, glossy and no longer sticky.

Add flour only as necessary; it is better to have a soft dough than a dry one.

Cover dough and leave in a warm place until doubled in size.

Put dough back on to a floured board and knead it for a second time, gently.

Shape into 2 round or oblong loaves.

Slash top of loaves several times with a sharp knife.

Put on baking tray, cover with a clean, damp tea towel and prove until risen and puffy.

Mix 1 tsp salt with 125ml water, and brush this over the loaves.

Sprinkle with caraway seeds/oats/sesame seeds.

Bake for approximately 45 minutes or until the loaves sound hollow when tapped.

Cool on wire tray.

Method using a breadmaker

If you have a breadmaker, use the manufacturer's instructions to mix and prove the dough and, after it has risen, take it out and follow the instructions above from the second kneading.

_____

Tip

_____

Look at the loaf sitting proudly on my stove in the cover photo of this book to see the finished article!

Challah (known in Austria as Barches) — Plaited Bread Loaf (traditional Jewish bread)

A rather special loaf which is coiled, and to my family signifies the beginning of the weekend. I love to make it on a Friday, when I serve it with some of the dishes I have described in the various sections of this book.

However humble the meal, with a glowing fresh loaf on the table, maybe a bottle of wine and some candles, one is ready to celebrate the end of a week and the promise of the weekend ahead.

Ingredients *(Makes 1 large or 2 smaller loaves)*
    500g strong white bread flour
    2 tsp salt
    2 tsp sugar
    1 tbs oil
    1½ tsp dried yeast or 25g fresh yeast
    1 large egg (or 2 small ones), beaten
    225ml warm water
    1 tsp poppy seeds or sesame seeds

Method
    Pre-heat oven to 225°C / gas mark 7.
    See method for Kümmelbrot (wholemeal seeded bread) for the first stage, but add beaten egg to the warm water.
    When dough has risen, turn onto floured board.
    Knead gently.
    Cut into 3 portions.
    Knead each one into a sausage 5cm x 24cm, rolling and stretching as you smooth it.
    Starting in the middle, plait it 2 or 3 times, tucking the ends underneath.
    Proceed in the same way for the other side.
    Cover, and put into a warm place to prove.

When well risen, brush with egg wash, sprinkle with seeds and bake until a rich brown, and hollow-sounding when tapped.

Cool on wire tray.

Tip

When beating the egg, put a small amount into a dish, add 1 tbs of water, and use it as the egg wash.

Gerührter Guglhupf – Sponge Guglhupf

There is no literal translation for this cake; the closest relative would be a Madeira cake. It is the special cake mould which makes it unique, ensuring a perfectly golden finish. (See also the recipe for Germguglhupf on page 188.) The usual simple decoration consists of some almonds (put into the tin before the dough) and a generous sprinkling of vanilla-flavoured icing sugar.

There are numerous recipes for Guglhupf. The one I am giving here is the most versatile. I have named it Regina Guglhupf after one of my best friends, who shared many recipes with me. The quantities here are for a 24cm tin, but a smaller cake can be made by halving the quantities and using 2 eggs instead of 3.

Ingredients

225g butter or soft margarine
225g caster sugar
325g self-raising flour
pinch of salt
1 level tsp baking powder
3 large eggs, beaten
grated zest and juice of 1 lemon
2 tbs sultanas or mixed dried fruit (can be soaked in rum or sherry)
25g blanched almonds or split almonds

Method

Pre-heat oven to 190°C / gas mark 5 and grease a large (24cm) tin.

Sprinkle inside of tin with fine breadcrumbs or flour, and arrange almonds all around the flutes.

Cream fat and sugar until light and fluffy.

Sift flour and baking powder.

Add eggs gradually to creamed fat, adding the occasional tablespoon of flour to avoid mixture curdling.

Fold in remaining flour. Do this very gently to maintain the fluffy consistency.

Add dried fruit, lemon zest and juice.

Pour into mould and bake for approximately 50 minutes.

Insert a skewer to check if cooked. If it comes out clean, remove from oven and leave for 10 minutes in mould.

Turn out by putting the cooling tray on top of the mould, and turning it upside down.

Leave to cool before sprinkling it liberally with icing sugar.

Marble Guglhupf

To make a Marble Guglhupf, use the previous recipe but omit the dried fruit. Put half the plain mixture into the bottom of the mould and to the other half add the following:

Ingredients

1 dsp cocoa

1 level tsp bicarbonate of soda

75ml milk and 1 tsp lemon juice (or the equivalent amount of plain yoghurt)

Method

Blend all ingredients together until smooth. Add to the remaining dough and stir well.

Spoon this on top of the plain mixture which is already in the Guglhupf mould.

Take a fork, insert it deeply into the two mixtures in several places and swirl it round.

Bake as above.

Tip

These cakes freeze very successfully, but don't sprinkle on the icing sugar until ready to serve.

Biskuit – Fatless Sponge

One of the most versatile recipes in my repertoire, Biskuit is quick and almost foolproof. The sponge can be used for simple jam-filled sandwich cakes, fruit flans, Swiss rolls, Indianerkrapfen (see page 207) – the list could almost be endless. It is also one of the few fat-free recipes, and used to be regarded as excellent food for invalids.

Most of us have some sort of egg whipping gadget, be it a mixing machine, hand-held electric beater or a rotary whisk. One of these is almost essential. I have been told that my grandmother made this cake by beating the eggs with two forks, which not only takes time but also a lot of energy. Therefore it was only made when one of the family was ill.

When I make this recipe, I always make double the quantity – one for immediate use and one for the freezer. Well wrapped up, it will keep without detriment for several weeks. The quantity below is for one sandwich cake, a 25cm flan, or one Swiss roll.

Ingredients

    3 eggs, separated
    175g caster sugar
    175g self-raising flour
    pinch of salt
    grated zest of one lemon, or vanilla essence

Method

    Pre-heat oven to 190°C / gas mark 5.

    Thoroughly grease two 20cm sandwich tins, or one 25cm flan tin. Line base with baking parchment.

    Sift flour.

    Whip egg whites until stiff, adding the sugar in spoonfuls whilst whisking.

    Add egg yolks and lemon zest, whisking until mixture is pale yellow.

    Fold in sifted flour. This must be done very gently but thoroughly with a large spoon, as flour gets trapped in air pockets which would spoil the cake.

    Add 1 tbs boiling water at the end.

Put into hot oven, bake for approximately 15 minutes until cake feels firm in the middle.

Leave in tin for 15 minutes before turning out onto cooling tray.

You can fill this sponge with jam, jam and whipped cream, lemon curd, or a creative concoction of your own!

Fruit flan

I tend to make this on a flat sponge base. Flan tins are available. They have a raised edge, and will give the original flan shape. They do tend to stick unless you buy a Teflon-coated one.

Ingredients

1 flan base made with the Biskuit recipe (see page 201)
500g strawberries
150ml whipping cream
1 tbs sieved apricot or strawberry jam

Method

Arrange halved strawberries over flan base.

Brush with melted, sieved jam (or use commercial flan gel).

Decorate with whipped cream.

Nussroulade –
Swiss Roll with Nut Cream Filling

Making a Swiss roll is not difficult. It is one of my grandson's favourites, and we have spent many happy times together in the kitchen baking them. At first he had to stand on a kitchen stool when he helped me roll them. Though they aren't difficult, there are some vital steps which must not be ignored. For instance, the oven must be hot, and the shelf placed fairly high. The oven tray has to be greased, and lined with baking parchment, snipped at the corners to make it fit. A second piece of baking paper must be ready, lightly floured, for the finished sponge to be turned over on.

Timing is crucial. The baking time is only about 7–9 minutes. The sponge must not be allowed to get hard around the edges.

Ingredients
1 quantity of the Biskuit recipe (page 201)

Filling
100g ground walnuts
75g caster sugar
approximately 3 tbs milk

Method
Pre-heat oven to 200°C / gas mark 6 and grease a 22cm x 32cm oven tray (or Swiss roll tin).

Spread mixture, tapping the tin gently to even it out.

Put into the oven, and look at it after 7 minutes.

When golden and firm, remove from oven.

Turn it upside down onto the floured paper.

Cut a third piece of paper.

Carefully remove the baking parchment from the sponge.

Put the third piece of paper on top of sponge.

Roll up from the long side nearest to you, leaving the paper inside (to be removed later).

All this should be done quite quickly, whilst the sponge is still warm.

Lift roll onto a cooling tray.

To make nut filling, put all filling ingredients into a pan, and heat gently until the mixture reaches spreading consistency. If you prefer, this can be done in the microwave for approximately 15 seconds.

When cake is cold, carefully unroll, and fill with nut filling.

Tip

Alternative fillings can be jam, raspberries and whipped cream, or anything that takes your fancy.

Savarin – Rum-soaked Sponge

The authentic Savarin is made with yeast, being of Russian origin, where yeast baking is more commonplace. This is a cheat version! I have found this method very good. It is always a hit with friends and family.

It can be made in a deep 20cm cake tin, but the original Savarin tin is round, with a hole in the middle.

Ingredients

1 quantity of Biskuit sponge mixture (page 201)

Syrup

100g sugar
275ml water
juice of 1 lemon
2 tbs dark rum

Decoration

split almonds or pistachio nuts and whipped cream

Method

Pre-heat oven to 190°C / gas mark 5. Grease and flour a suitable cake tin.

Put mixture into tin and bake for approximately 20 minutes, until firm and golden.

Turn onto cooling tray and allow to cool. When cooled put onto serving plate.

In the meantime, prepare the syrup as follows:

Put water and sugar into a small pan.

Dissolve slowly, then boil for 10 minutes without stirring. Do *not* let it caramelise.

Add lemon juice and rum.

Pour the syrup over the sponge at once.

If a round Savarin tin has been used, the middle can be filled with fresh fruit salad.

The cake glistens with the syrup and is decorated with the split almonds or pistachio nuts. Swirls of whipped cream enhance it even further.

Indianerkrapfen – Chocolate-covered Buns

These buns, resplendent in their shiny, chocolatey, politically incorrectly named livery (the German means Indian buns), and oozing with whipped cream, can be seen in cafés and Konditoreien all over Austria. They also happen to be my husband's favourites, but sadly, for health reasons, they are now a rare treat. I have experimented with them, and have managed to get a reasonably professional result using somewhat unorthodox methods.

Ingredients

12 empty half eggshells, well oiled
1 quantity of Biskuit sponge mixture (page 201)
275ml whipping cream
1 tsp sugar
dark chocolate coating

Method

Pre-heat oven to 190°C / gas mark 5 and grease a 12-bun tray very thoroughly.

Divide mixture into bun tray.

Push a well-oiled half eggshell, open end up, into the middle of each 'bun'.

Bake for 12–15 minutes.

Remove from oven.

Carefully, with the help of a small knife, remove the (now brittle) eggshell. This leaves the hollow to be filled later.

Leave to cool.

Whip cream until stiff, adding sugar towards the end.

Fill one bun generously with cream and then put another, upside down, on top.

Melt chocolate coating as directed on package, and cover the top bun.

Sachertorte – Rich Chocolate Cake

This is without doubt the most famous Torte in Vienna, and even in other countries many people have at least heard the name. Viennese bakeries and hotels have for decades competed with each other in order to produce the perfect product. Indeed, two major gastronomic concerns, Hotel Sacher and Café Demel, have been litigating against each other (and I believe still are) as to which of them is entitled to be recognised as the one and only true purveyor of the Sachertorte. Legend has it that the point at issue is whether the original recipe included a layer of jam in the middle, or not.

I have been sent an original Sachertorte by post, and though the Schokolade Glasur – the shiny, smooth dark chocolate coating – was outstanding, the cake itself was, to my mind, rather dry and disappointing. But of course, it had been posted several days previously, which may have accounted for its dryness. The following recipe has been used by my family for all special occasions, and it works. It is as near to the precious (and secret) original recipe as I can get.

Ingredients

100g caster sugar
100g butter
5 large eggs, separated
100g ground almonds
100g dark chocolate of high cocoa content, about 60–70%
40g breadcrumbs (or digestive biscuit crumbs)
1 tsp baking powder
1 tbs dark rum or sherry

Coating

sieved apricot jam
chocolate icing (see page 210)

Method

Pre-heat oven to 190°C / gas mark 5 (to be reduced after 15 minutes baking to 180°C / gas mark 4. Total baking time is 45 minutes.)

Grease and line a 20cm cake tin, preferably loose based.

Put chocolate into a double pan to melt. (Do not let it touch the hot water.)

Cream half the sugar with butter.

Add egg yolks, cream until pale and thick, add rum.

Add the cooled but liquid chocolate.

Add breadcrumbs, ground almonds, and baking powder.

Whisk 5 egg whites until stiff, folding in the remaining sugar whilst whisking.

Fold egg whites very gently into the chocolate mixture.

Pour into greased and lined tin and bake for 15 minutes at higher temperature and 30 minutes at lower temperature.

Insert a skewer to see if cooked; the top of the cake should feel firm.

Allow to cool for 10 minutes before turning it out onto a baking tray.

When cold, spread top and sides with heated, sieved apricot jam.

Tip

A double pan is a basin balanced over a pan of boiling water so that the contents are melted without contact with the water.

Schokolade Glasur – Chocolate Icing

For more years than I care to mention, I have tried to make the perfect Chocolate Glasur, and I have never been able to achieve a truly professional result. Chocolate is a very difficult medium to work with, and although the relatively cheap chocolate cake covering gives a good visual result, it seems heavy and not suitable for a Sachertorte. So, to save you the disappointments I have had, I am giving you the following recipe, which I have found to look good and to taste superb, alas without having the hard finish of the original.

Ingredients
   200ml double cream
   200g dark chocolate (70% cocoa solids)

Method
   Melt chocolate in double pan.

   When cool, add cream.

   Stir to mix.

   Pour over the cake and spread it round the sides. The less you touch the top, the better.

   Leave to set. Sachertorte is generally left plain, but you could decorate it with a few browned almonds or walnuts.

   Serve with whipped cream by the side.

Nusstorte – Nut Gâteau

Continental cakes frequently contain ground nuts in varying quantities, and consequently contain less flour. This alters the consistency, making it lighter and more moist. The following recipe contains no flour, is suitable for people with a gluten allergy, and is eaten by observant Jewish families at Passover, a time when ritual forbids the use of flour. Whatever your health or religious orientation, it is delicious.

Ingredients

100g walnuts or hazelnuts (ground almonds are not suitable)
100g caster sugar
4 large eggs, separated and kept at room temperature

Decoration

150ml double or whipping cream
½ tsp sugar
a few walnut halves or raspberries

Method

Pre-heat oven to 180°C / gas mark 4. Grease and bottom-line a 20cm cake tin.

Grind nuts using a coffee grinder or food processor.

Beat egg whites until stiff, adding sugar gradually whilst beating.

Add egg yolks one at a time and continue beating.

Fold in ground nuts. Do this very gently to maintain the fluffy consistency.

Pour into prepared tin, bake in the middle of the oven for approximately 40 minutes.

When cooked, leave in tin for 10 minutes to settle before turning out onto cooling tray. The cake will sink a little due to its soufflé-like texture.

Continued overleaf

Whip cream to piping consistency, adding sugar part way through whipping.

Cover cake with whipped cream, decorate with a fork, and arrange walnuts or raspberries on top.

Tip

The flavour of the nuts is improved if put into the oven for 5 minutes before grinding. But beware – they burn very easily.

Haselnusstorte – Hazelnut Meringue Gâteau

This is a very special cake for my family. I made it to celebrate the birth of one of my granddaughters. It was a home birth, and my husband and I got an SOS to get to Sheffield in order to look after the other two siblings, then aged 6 and 4.

Complete with a ready-prepared and frozen cake, and all the other necessary paraphernalia, we hurried along. A healthy baby duly arrived several hours later, and the cake was taken to the bedroom of the proud mother and placed on a chair near the bed. The doctor arrived and promptly almost sat on it. It is a very light, frothy confection, and it was just saved in time.

Ingredients

    4 egg whites
    250g caster sugar
    ½ tsp vanilla essence
    ½ tsp vinegar
    150g ground hazelnuts
    150ml whipping cream (extra if you intend to decorate the top)
    150g raspberries, or other soft fruit, to decorate

Method

    Pre-heat oven to 190°C / gas mark 5 and grease, line and flour two 20cm sandwich tins.

    Whisk egg whites.

    Add sugar, 1 tbs at a time whilst whisking.

    Beat until very stiff, and add vanilla essence and vinegar (this keeps meringue soft).

    Fold in ground hazelnuts.

    Divide mixture between the two tins and bake for 35 to 40 minutes.

    When firm on top, cool in tins for 5 minutes.

    Turn out and remove paper carefully. Cool.

    Whip cream, adding ½ tsp sugar part way through whipping.

    Mix raspberries with whipped cream and use as filling between the two layers.

    Decorate top with sprinkled icing sugar and swirls of whipped cream.

Linzertorte –
Hazelnut or Almond Shortbread with Jam

Note that this can be made into individual Linzertörtchen (single portion pastries – see opposite).

Linz is the capital of Upper Austria, an industrial city of no great distinction. I must admit that I do not know why it is famous for this delicious confection, but I can vouch for its sumptuousness and attractive appearance.

Ingredients
150g firm butter (soft margarine will not do)
150g flour (half plain, half self-raising)
150g caster sugar
100g ground almonds or hazelnuts
1 egg, separated
1 tsp lemon juice
pinch of cinnamon and pinch of ground cloves
raspberry, redcurrant or Morello cherry jam

Method
Pre-heat oven to 190°C / gas mark 5.

Grease a 25cm loose-based shallow baking tin (or Swiss roll tin for sliced portions).

Rub butter into flour until consistency is like breadcrumbs.

Add sugar, ground almonds and spices.

Add egg yolk and lemon juice.

Put mixture on a board and knead to get pliable consistency.

Wrap in clingfilm and refrigerate for 30 minutes.

Remove pastry from fridge, divide in half.

Roll half pastry to fit base of tin and place in tin.

Brush with egg white (to avoid sogginess).

Cover the pastry with jam to within 1cm of the edge.

Roll the remaining pastry into 1cm sausage. Press this round the edge.

Make a lattice (criss-cross) pattern with strips of pastry to go over the top.

Brush this with egg white.

Put into the oven to bake until nicely brown, approximately 40 minutes.

Linzerschnitten – Hazelnut or Almond Pastry Slices

If made in a Swiss roll tin, cut into slices when cool. These are called Linzerschnitten.

Linzertörtchen – Tartlets

You can make this into individual tartlets as follows.

Cut 24 circles with a 4cm or 5cm tartlet cutter.

Leave 12 of these whole, cutting a 1cm circle (or other shape) from the middle of the remaining 12.

Bake at 190°C / gas mark 5 for 20 minutes.

When cooked, add jam to the complete circles and sprinkle the top ones (with the hole) liberally with icing sugar before sandwiching them together.

Schokoladetorte –
The Ultimate Chocolate Gâteau

After working my way through dozens of chocolate cakes, from Sachertorte to Devil's Food Cake, I came across this cake on a visit to my cousin. Eating it was quite a revelation. It was moist, a deep dark chocolate colour, economical, delicious, and, most importantly, it has never failed. I have made this cake for many occasions. It has been an 18th, 21st, 40th, 50th, 65th, 80th and 90th birthday cake, and I have handed out dozens of copies of the recipe. This cake is made in two stages. Note that the praline cream should be made in advance.

First stage:

Ingredients

   75g sugar
   6 tbs water
   60g cocoa powder
   175ml milk

Method

   Put sugar, cocoa and water into a pan.

   Heat and stir until consistency is smooth.

   Add milk. Leave to cool.

Second stage:

Ingredients

   225g caster sugar
   225g softened butter or margarine
   4 large eggs, separated
   225g self-raising flour
   2 tsp baking powder
   pinch of salt
   1 tsp vanilla essence

Method

Pre-heat oven to 180°C / gas mark 4. Grease and line a 25cm cake tin.

Cream butter and sugar until white and fluffy.

Add egg yolks and vanilla essence.

Sift flour, baking powder and salt.

Add cooled cocoa mixture, alternating with spoonfuls of flour.

Fold in remaining flour.

Whisk egg whites until stiff.

Fold in gently but thoroughly.

Pour the mixture into the cake tin.

Bake for approximately 45 minutes.

Leave 5 minutes before turning out onto cooling tray.

Leave until cold and spread with the following:

Praline Cream:

Ingredients

125ml double cream
100g plain chocolate
1 tbs rum or brandy or strong coffee

Method

Put cream into a pan.

Add chocolate.

Heat slowly until dissolved.

Add rum or coffee, stir.

Cool then cover.

Leave in fridge overnight.

Whisk until light and fluffy. It is now ready to spread.

Biskottentorte – Refrigerator Tipsy Cake

The Viennese answer to the English trifle or the Italian Tiramisu. All you need is some good rum and strong coffee.

Ingredients

1 packet sponge fingers
135ml very strong coffee
2 tbs dark rum

Hazelnut cream

50g dark chocolate
50g butter
50g ground hazelnuts
1 egg yolk
50g icing sugar
125ml whipping cream

Method

Line the base of a 1kg loaf tin with foil.

Melt chocolate with butter in double pan.

Add ground hazelnuts, sugar and egg yolk.

Beat mixture until the consistency is light and creamy.

Put coffee and rum into a wide bowl, dip in one sponge finger at a time, and fit side by side closely together.

Cover this layer with the cream.

Repeat several layers, finishing with sponge fingers.

Cover with greaseproof paper and press down.

Leave in fridge for several hours, or overnight.

Turn out, cover with stiffly whipped cream.

Decorate with grated chocolate and/or chopped nuts.

Cut into slices to serve.

Kastanientorte – Chestnut Gâteau

Chestnuts are always associated with autumn and bonfire night, and my family love to roast chestnuts. I take advantage of their enthusiasm and get them to roast a few extra, enabling me to make the following Torte. But I do have a cheat version, using chestnut purée or preserved chestnuts, which are available in delicatessen shops or larger supermarkets. If you are using fresh chestnuts, slit and roast them in a hot oven for about 10 minutes. Peel them, put them into boiling water and simmer until soft. Drain, and grind or purée.

Ingredients

300g cooked and puréed chestnuts, or a tin of chestnut purée
150g caster sugar
4 eggs, separated
100g cocoa powder
1 dsp fine breadcrumbs
1 tbs hot water
1 tsp vanilla essence
200ml whipping cream
18cm lined cake tin (preferably with a loose base)

Method

Pre-heat oven to 190°C / gas mark 5.

Beat egg yolks and vanilla essence with half of the sugar.

Add cocoa powder, breadcrumbs, chestnut purée and water.

Beat egg whites until stiff, adding sugar gradually whilst beating.

Fold egg whites very gently into chestnut mixture.

Put into cake tin. Bake for approximately 50 minutes.

When firm on top and skewer comes out clean, leave for 10 minutes in tin to cool.

Turn onto cooling tray.

This cake will sink slightly in the middle, due to its light texture.

Whip the cream until stiff, and decorate the cake with it when cold.

Tip

A few halved chestnuts arranged on top make an attractive finish.

Weihnachtliche Leckerbissen –
Christmas Treats

Despite our Jewish roots, Christmas is an annual celebration in our family.
It provides an opportunity for us all to pause a while in the busyness of
our daily lives and to gather together to enjoy each others' company
and, of course, *food*! We eat both traditional English Christmas fare and
Weihnachtliche Spezialitäten.

Vanillekipferln – Vanilla Crescents

These are the essential biscuits in most Austrian homes at Christmas time. In popularity they are the equivalent of English mince pies, although in reality there is no similarity, except that both are sweet. I recently spent a few days in Vienna just prior to Christmas, and visited several friends and relatives. Hospitality abounded, but wherever I went, a platter of Vanillekipferln appeared, and I began to crave for something savoury!

They are made without the addition of liquid or egg, relying on the butter content and quantity of hazelnuts. They take a bit of practice to shape. All my grandchildren have in their time stood next to me and produced tray after tray, always being the first to taste the quality of their produce.

Ingredients

150g caster sugar
175g hazelnuts – do not remove husk
200g butter at room temperature (sorry, margarine will not do)
250g plain flour
1 tsp vanilla essence
extra sugar (preferably vanilla flavoured)

Method

Pre-heat oven to 180°C / gas mark 4 and lightly grease 2 flat baking trays.

Grind hazelnuts (or buy ready ground).

Rub butter into flour until fine crumbs are formed.

Add hazelnuts.

Add sugar.

Add vanilla essence.

Knead this mixture until it becomes smooth and pliable, working on a cool surface.

Roll into 5cm-diameter sausage, then cut into 6 portions.

Now take one portion at a time, and roll into pencil-thick sausage.

Cut into 5cm lengths and shape into a crescent.

Put on baking tray, allowing a little space between them.

Bake in oven for approximately 15 minutes. They must not get brown. Aim for the colour of shortbread.

Remove from oven, allow just 5 minutes to cool.

Have a sheet of kitchen towel ready on a plate, covered with a cupful of vanilla-flavoured caster sugar.

Toss the Kipferln in the sugar whilst still warm.

Cool on wire tray, store in an airtight tin or jar.

Tip

These biscuits are very brittle at this stage, which results in a few breakages. This in turn allows for a few tasty nibbles, which can easily lead to an addiction!

Bischof Keks – Nut and Chocolate Crisps

These little biscuits were offered to me on a fairly recent visit to a friend who lives in St Pölten, near Vienna. We had shared some very important years during the war in a small cotton-mill town in Lancashire, having worked in the same mill, and our fathers regularly enjoyed a game of Tarock (an Austrian card game) together. Elsa returned to Austria after the war, but we have remained in close contact throughout the years. She has been generous not only with her friendship, but also with her recipes.

These biscuits are a wonderful addition to the usual Christmas fare, and if not eaten straight away they will keep almost indefinitely. Serve them with coffee, sloe gin or hot punch (Glühwein – see page 243).

Ingredients

2 eggs
125g caster sugar
175g plain flour, plus a bit extra for working with
100g hazelnuts, left whole
50g plain chocolate, chopped
1 lemon, zest only
1 tbs fine breadcrumbs (if necessary)

Method

Pre-heat oven to 170°C / gas mark 3 and well grease a baking tray.

Beat eggs.

Add sugar and beat lightly.

Add sieved flour.

Add all other ingredients.

Mixture should be of scone-like consistency.

If too sloppy, add breadcrumbs and a little flour.

Roll into 2 sausages, 6cm in diameter.

Put onto the baking tray.

Bake for approximately 30 minutes.

Cool on cooling tray.

When cold, cut into thin slices with a sharp knife. Store in a biscuit tin.

Basler Leckerle – Swiss Spiced Biscuits

After a lifetime's search for the perfect Lebzelten (spiced biscuits), I was served a plate of these delicious cookies during a lesson of patch-working. The teacher was a remarkable old lady with numerous skills who, amongst her other talents, had been a home economist in Switzerland during her youth. She kindly gave me this recipe, which I am happy to pass on.

Ingredients

½ cup honey
½ cup sugar
¾ cup chopped candied peel
1 tsp grated lemon zest
1 cup blanched split almonds
2 cups sifted plain flour
½ tsp ground cloves
1 tsp ground nutmeg
1 tsp cinnamon
1 tsp bicarbonate of soda
¼ cup water

Coating

½ cup sugar
¼ cup water

Method

Pre-heat oven to 150°C / gas mark 2 and well grease 2 flat baking trays.

Heat honey, sugar and water in a large saucepan until warm and melted.

Remove from heat.

Add remaining ingredients when lukewarm.

Sift flour, spices and bicarbonate of soda.

Add to ingredients in pan, and mix.

Wrap the dough in clingfilm, put into fridge to mellow.

Leave for 2 days.

Remove from fridge, roll to thickness of £1 coin. Cut into desired shapes.

This quantity makes approximately 56 biscuits.

Cool on cooling tray before coating with icing.

To make coating, bring sugar and water to the boil.

Boil until liquid thickens. (Do not let it colour.)

Brush onto biscuits. This will form the authentic shiny glaze.

Tip

When cold, store in airtight tin. If you also put a small apple in the tin, the biscuits will remain in perfect condition.

Kastanien Schokolade Roulade – Chestnut Cream Log

Our Christmas dinner is always a happy gathering of the clan, and amongst the 20 or so guests, there are several fads to be catered for. The Christmas pudding, a true English version, is loved by some and judged annually by comparison with previous examples, like fine wine. For those who do not like it, the chestnut log is always one of the tasty alternatives.

Ingredients

Roulade (Swiss roll)
   3 large eggs, separated
   75g self-raising flour
   pinch of salt
   75g caster sugar
   1 tsp cocoa mixed with 1 tbs water
   ½ tsp vanilla essence

Filling and coating
   400g tin chestnut purée
   2 tbs rum or brandy (or orange juice if intended for children)
   100g icing sugar
   50g softened butter

Method

   Pre-heat oven to 200°C / gas mark 6 and line a Swiss roll tin with baking parchment.

   Beat egg whites until stiff. Fold in sugar gradually.

   Add egg yolks whilst continuing to whisk.

   Mixture should be white and leave a trail when lifted with a spoon.

   Add the cocoa and vanilla.

   Finally, very gently and thoroughly fold in the sifted flour.

   Pour into lined Swiss roll tin and bake on a high shelf until firm to the touch.

Tip upside down onto a sheet of ready prepared, lightly floured greaseproof paper.

Carefully remove lining paper from the cake. Cover cake with another sheet of paper, and roll up from the long side nearest to you, leaving the paper inside (to be removed later).

All this should be done quite quickly, whilst the sponge is still warm.

Cool on wire tray.

To make filling, beat chestnut purée with butter and icing sugar.

Add rum or orange juice gradually, beating until smooth.

Divide mixture in half, using half to fill the cooled roll (paper now removed), trimming the edges of the cake diagonally.

For a topping, spread the remaining filling all over.

Using a fork, mark lines across the top, and swirls round the diagonal cuts.

Decorate with grated chocolate, or marzipan holly leaves.

Weihnachtsstollen

No translation is needed: this cake, originally native to Germany and Austria, has become a very well-known addition to our annual Christmas fare. In England it is usually known simply as Stollen, but in Austria the full name, Weihnachtsstollen, distinguishes it from Osterstollen (Easter Stollen), which is spicy and does not have the marzipan filling. Weihnachtsstollen are readily available in many supermarkets, and vary in price from very cheap to extraordinarily expensive. It is always reasonably good, but it can also be exquisite. You usually get what you pay for.

It is debatable whether it is worth going to the trouble of making Stollen, but I find it easy, enjoy the effort, and always make a large quantity. Stollen make excellent presents. They keep well, freeze well, and I can choose what ingredients to use.

Ingredients *(For 2 Stollen)*
>   450g mixed fruit
>   50g chopped almonds
>   2 tbs rum or brandy or sherry
>   450g flour (half strong white and half plain)
>   ½ tsp salt
>   175g butter or soft margarine
>   100g sugar
>   2 large eggs
>   150ml warm milk
>   25g fresh yeast or 1½ tsp dried yeast

Filling
>   225g marzipan

Topping
>   50g unsalted butter melted
>   50g icing sugar

Method

Use a flat, well-greased baking tray.

Stage 1

Wash fruit. Allow to dry for 24 hours.

Soak fruit in spirit.

Sift flour into large bowl. Add salt.

Beat eggs.

Melt butter. Allow to cool.

Make hollow into the flour, add yeast.

Pour a little of the warm milk onto the yeast. N.B. Do not heat milk above body temperature, as too much heat kills the yeast.

Allow yeast to dissolve.

Add eggs, sugar, butter and remaining milk.

Beat mixture until combined.

Turn onto a floured board and knead until smooth and silky. (If you have a breadmaker all this could be done by the machine.)

Put the dough into a large, oiled bowl and cover.

Put it in a warm, draught-free place. Leave until doubled in size.

Stage 2

Pre-heat oven to 200°C / gas mark 6.

Turn the risen dough onto a floured board. Add the dried fruit, then knead gently until distributed.

Divide dough in half. Roll one half into an oblong.

Roll the marzipan into a 2cm sausage. Put half the marzipan sausage into the middle of the dough.

Fold the dough over the marzipan. Press into a half-moon shape.

Put on greased baking tray.

Repeat with second half.

Bake for approximately 40 minutes.

Remove from oven, and immediately brush with melted butter.

Sprinkle liberally with icing sugar.

Cool on cooling tray.

Christmas Cake

This is the recipe I was given during my very first year at a catering college, which I attended as a part-time student and which fired me with the enthusiasm that lasted a lifetime. The lecturer was a very old-fashioned lady of rather unusual physical proportions – a real Lancashire woman with an amazing ability to enthuse her students and impart sound knowledge. Until then I had never made a Christmas cake, having been loyal instead to my familiar traditional Austrian goodies.

The cake was a revelation to my family and I have made it to the same recipe for the last 45 years. My children and grandchildren automatically go to the internet for recipes, and I have had no requests for this one, but nevertheless here goes! I do make it at the beginning of November, giving it time to mature.

This quantity fills a 20cm square tin or a 23cm round tin.

Ingredients

  225g butter
  225g sugar
  4 large eggs, beaten
  225g plain flour
  1 level tsp salt
  ½ level tsp mixed spice
  450g sultanas
  325g currants
  50g cherries chopped
  50g candied peel
  50g ground almonds
  50g nibbed almonds (skinned almonds chopped into pieces about 2mm square)
  125ml brandy or rum or sherry (or fruit juice for non-alcohol drinkers)

Method

Stage 1

Put all dried fruit into a sieve and wash with lots of warm water.

Spread fruit out on a flat tray and allow to dry. (This is important to remove extra sugar and plump up the fruit.)

Pour the spirit onto the fruit, mix well, then leave overnight to absorb.

Stage 2

Pre-heat the oven to 180°C / gas mark 4.

Sift flour and spices together.

Cream butter and sugar until fluffy.

Add beaten eggs gradually, interspersed with a little flour.

Fold in remaining flour, gently but thoroughly.

Add ground almonds and all the fruit.

Pour into greased, double-lined tin.

Level mixture, but make a dip in the centre. This will ensure a fairly even top.

Tie double thickness brown parcel paper round the cake tin.

Put a double thickness of brown paper onto a baking tray. (Do not let it overlap.)

Put the cake tin on top. (The paper stops the cake hardening at the bottom and edges).

Bake, following instructions overleaf. Check after 2 hours: if the top is getting brown, put a piece of greaseproof paper over.

Test with a skewer, which must come out clean. If not, bake a little longer.

Remove when ready. Do not remove from tin until the following day.

Do not remove the paper until ready to be iced, but store in an airtight tin, fortnightly dribbling a spoon of spirit over the top. (This is optional but highly recommended!)

The cake can then be coated with jam, marzipan and icing, or just covered with an array of candied fruit and nuts and then glazed with warmed, sieved apricot jam.

Baking instructions

Put in pre-heated oven (180°C / gas mark 4) for 15 minutes.

Reduce to 170°C / gas mark 3 for 1½ hours.

Reduce to 150°C / gas mark 2 for 2 further hours.

(Total baking time approximately 3 hours 45 minutes).

Alternatively, since modern ovens are thermostatically controlled, you can achieve good results at a steady temperature of 140°C / gas mark 1 for the full baking time. Consult your oven instructions.

Christmas Pudding

We are constantly bombarded with old and new recipes, and updates of traditional fare. I have stayed with this particular recipe, which was given to me by a fellow dedicated home economist many years ago, and I am happy to share it with you in the hope that one day one of my grandchildren – or maybe their partners – will want to make it. This is another recipe which is far better if allowed to mature, so the earlier you can make it, the better. I often keep one for the following year.

Ingredients (*Makes 1 large or 2 medium puddings*)

700g dried fruit or a mixture of raisins, currants, sultanas, and muscatel raisins.
150ml brown ale
50g glacé cherries
50g candied peel
50g split almonds
2 eggs
1 large grated apple
1 large grated carrot
grated zest and juice of 1 orange
grated zest and juice of 1 lemon
¼ tsp nutmeg
½ tsp mixed spice
75g self-raising flour
75g demerara sugar
175g fresh breadcrumbs (made from slightly stale bread, crusts removed)
225g suet (can be vegetarian)
1 dsp treacle

Method

Wash and dry fruit overnight.
Soak in ale for 24 hours.
Sift all dry ingredients together.
Beat eggs, add fruit juice.
Mix fruit, carrot, apple, and grated zest together in a large bowl.

Add dry ingredients and suet.

Mix thoroughly. (I do this with my hands, finding it more efficient than with a spoon.)

Put mixture into a greased pudding basin, only filling the basin three-quarters full.

Cover with greaseproof paper or tin foil which has a 2cm pleat in the middle to allow for expansion.

Secure covering with string.

Steam for approximately 6 hours. (Do not let steamer boil dry. Keep adding boiling water as necessary.)

Remove from steamer and take off wrapping.

When cold, leave in pudding basin to reheat on the day, but cover with paper and foil.

Store in a dry, cool place.

To serve

Steam for a further 3 hours, then loosen pudding gently in the basin with a palette knife and turn onto a warm plate. Prepare a rum sauce (see next recipe).

Rum Sauce

The secret is in the quantity of rum used in the sauce. I always use the Austrian 80% vol. rum, which has a very pungent taste and is dark in colour.

Ingredients *(Makes about 300ml Sauce)*
- 275ml milk
- 1 level tbs cornflour
- 1 level dsp sugar
- 2 tbs rum
- 20g butter
- 1–2 tbs rum or brandy for flaming

Method

Put milk, sugar and cornflour into a heavy small pan.

Bring to boil, stirring constantly in a figure of 8. This avoids it burning and being lumpy.

As soon as the mixture is thick enough to coat the spoon, take it off the heat.

Add butter and rum, and stir.

If waiting (i.e. not serving immediately), put a piece of clingfilm directly onto the sauce, which will prevent it from forming a skin.

Just before serving the pudding, heat rum or brandy for a minute or so, light it and pour over the pudding, flames and all. Check your house insurance first! I cannot give this recipe without confessing to an accident a few years ago, which could easily have turned into a catastrophe.

The family were making merry in the dining room, patiently waiting for the pudding. I lit the brandy in the kitchen, and as I carried the pudding to the table, the spirit spilled over onto the carpet, setting it on fire. Luckily my daughter heard my shriek and together we trampled out the flames. Fortunately the damage was restricted to the hall carpet. The insurers were astonished at the reason for our claim – it was the first claim they had ever had as a result of a Christmas pudding accident! So...

Tip

Put the pudding on the table, take the warmed spirit to the table separately, pour it over the pudding, and then, and only then, put a match to it!

Miscellany

Many of these recipes are seasonal, using ingredients which capture the spirit of a particular time of year.

Elderflower Cordial –
Hollersirup (Holunderblütensirup)

This refreshing drink is known as Hollersirup in Austria and Holunderblütensirup in Germany. Although it's a summer drink, if frozen in a plastic container, it can be enjoyed the year round. I love making it with the elderflowers growing in the lane outside our house. I always associate elderflower cordial with a sunny summer's day.

Ingredients

25 elderflower heads
1kg sugar
2 lemons
2 oranges
40g citric acid
1 litre boiling water

Method

Squeeze oranges and lemons.
Wash peel, cut into rough chunks.
Put fruit, juice, sugar, and citric acid in a large bowl.
Pour boiling water over mixture.
Stir until sugar and citric acid have dissolved.
Leave to stand for 4 days.
Strain through muslin.
Put into bottles and store in fridge or freeze.

Tip

Citric acid is obtainable from chemists. They may ask for assurance that you are using it for culinary purposes.

Lemon Squash

Home-made lemon squash is a far cry from the commercially available product.

It is the perfect drink to have available in summer, and from June to September there is always a bottle in my fridge. Served with ice and some fresh fruit, and maybe a mint leaf, it's a drink with a difference.

Ingredients
3 lemons
1kg sugar
1 litre boiling water
50g tartaric acid (available from chemists)

Method
Peel lemons thinly (leaving the pith behind).

Squeeze lemon juice.

Put lemon peel and sugar into a large jug. Pour boiling water on top.

When sugar is dissolved, remove lemon rind.

When cool, add tartaric acid and juice from lemons.

Bottle and refrigerate.

Dilute to taste.

Tip

If you heat lemons slightly (microwave 10 seconds), you will get much more juice.

Sloe Gin

One of my favourite classes during my teaching career in adult education was a class for men. This seems very sexist now, but in the 1970s it was certainly needed, and quite unique. I saw a great need as I observed my male friends struggle when their partners became ill, or if they were widowed. I started the class with five men, but after 1 year there was a waiting list. Among the students there were chemists, a Reuters journalist and several doctors, all eager to learn basics such as making gravy after roasting a piece of meat, or making bread or Christmas cake.

It was the most rewarding work I ever did, and I was spoiled by all the men. This recipe for sloe gin was given to me by one of the chemists, and I have made it annually ever since. The 'secret' has now been passed on to my husband, who produces it in bulk. Everybody likes it so much that it finds an honoured place among the Christmas presents.

Ingredients (*Makes about ½ litre*)
    125g sloes (or damsons)
    175g sugar
    450ml gin

Method
    Prick or slit each sloe.
    Drop directly into an empty, sterilised spirit bottle.
    Add sugar and gin, put lid on the bottle.
    Agitate gently by inverting the bottle until sugar is dissolved. This will take time.
    For the next 2 weeks agitate daily, after that weekly.
    Allow to mature for 3 months.
    Decant carefully, by pouring through a sieve lined with muslin.

Tip

Put the fruit in the freezer overnight. This makes the berries burst, so you can omit the piercing. I tend to wrap the bottle in paper and put it in a safe place in the boot of the car – taking it for a ride agitates it very efficiently!

Glühwein – Mulled Wine

No book on Austrian cookery would be complete without a recipe for this invigorating and welcoming drink, to be served in the middle of winter.

Anybody who has ever been on a skiing holiday will have tasted Glühwein, either at the top of the slopes or in the village where there are stalls serving steaming little glasses. My frozen hands as well as my taste buds have always greatly appreciated this traditional tipple. My experience of the ski slopes is limited, but I always serve Glühwein as a welcoming drink at Christmas, on New Year's Eve, and on New Year's Day whilst listening to the Vienna Philharmonic New Year's Day concert and wishing everyone Prosit Neu Jahr!

Ingredients

1 litre inexpensive red wine
4 tbs sugar
3cm piece of cinnamon stick
3 cloves
pinch of mace
thinly pared skin of 1 orange
125ml rum or brandy or vodka, added just before serving (optional)

Method

Heat the wine with all the other ingredients until warm, but do not let it boil.

Tip

If the Glühwein is rather hot when you pour it into the glasses, place a teaspoon in the glass to absorb some of the heat, thus avoiding cracks.

Powidl – Prune Jam (V)

Since this book contains the recipe for Germknödeln (see page 166), I need to include this special jam because it is difficult to purchase in Britain, unless you are lucky enough to live in an area with a delicatessen or Polish grocer. Powidl also makes a wonderful filling for pancakes, yeast crescents and many other pastries, and is divine spread on freshly baked bread or scones.

Ingredients

225g prunes (stoned)
100g sugar
½ tsp cinnamon

Method

Cover prunes with water. Soak overnight.

Simmer until soft in just enough liquid to cover.

Liquidise or whizz in food processor.

Add sugar and cinnamon.

Return to pan, cook gently for a further 5 minutes, until mixture is thick.

Put into clean jar and cover whilst hot.

It will keep in the fridge for up to 4 weeks.

Onion Marmalade (V)

I have had many requests for this relish, which has become popular in restaurants. I am therefore delighted to be able to pass the recipe on. It goes well with a cheese or cold meat platter.

Ingredients

500g red onions, chopped
1 tbs olive oil
75g light muscovado sugar
150ml red wine vinegar
salt and pepper to taste

Method

Heat oil.

Fry onion until soft.

Stir in vinegar and sugar.

Cook, uncovered, for 25–30 minutes, until caramelised, stirring occasionally.

Tip

This needs careful watching! It is perfect when just caramelised, but can be ruined if you don't catch it at the right stage.

Pikante Zucchini – Courgette Pickle (V)

This is an excellent way of using up those surplus courgettes which accumulate if one is a keen gardener, or has a generous friend who is. This recipe was given to me by a Hungarian friend. Not only was she a linguist who spoke seven languages, but she was also a wonderful cook, gardener and hostess, and we spent many happy hours exchanging recipes.

Ingredients *(Makes 8 x 225g jars)*
  1kg courgettes
  200g onions
  1 green pepper
  50g salt
  ½ litre wine or cider vinegar
  225g soft brown sugar
  1 level tsp turmeric
  ½ level tsp ground cloves
  2 dsp mustard seeds
  ½ tsp celery seeds

Method
  Slice courgettes as finely as you can (a food processor or mandolin is helpful).
  Slice onion and green pepper.
  Put into large enamel or glass bowl.
  Sprinkle salt over vegetables.
  Leave at least 3 hours.
  Drain, wash and squeeze out as much liquid as you can.
  Put into a large pan with vinegar.
  Add spices.
  Simmer until just tender ('al dente').
  Remove from heat, stir in sugar.
  Boil until sugar is dissolved.
  Whilst still hot, put into warm, sterilised jars.
  Cover tightly.

Mushroom and Tomato Sauce (V)

The excellent and ubiquitous Italian tomato sauce is frequently served with pasta and parmesan cheese, but the following recipe just has that extra something, which makes it a particularly satisfying vegetarian sauce for hardened meat eaters!

Ingredients

1 onion, chopped
1 dsp oil
2 cloves of garlic, crushed
225g mushrooms, washed and sliced
400g tin tomatoes
1 dsp tomato purée
200g light cream cheese
fresh basil leaves or ½ tsp dried oregano
salt and pepper
½ tsp sugar

Method

Fry onion until soft, then add garlic.

Add mushrooms and fry lightly.

Add tomatoes.

Season with salt, pepper and sugar.

Simmer gently for approximately 30 minutes.

Stir in the cream cheese, and reheat, but do not boil.

Tear a few leaves of basil, and sprinkle on top before serving.

Turkish Pickled Olives (V)

Not only did we spend a wonderful holiday in Turkey, in the home of one of our oldest friends, but we also came back with some outstandingly good honey, olive oil and this recipe for making quite ordinary, cheap olives taste exceptionally good.

Ingredients

1 jar of black or green olives, strained
2 or 3 cloves of garlic, sliced
1 lemon
1 tsp chilli flakes (or a pinch of chilli powder)
1 tsp dried oregano
good quality olive oil

Method

Put olives into a glass or porcelain dish.

Add the juice of the lemon.

Add the sliced garlic.

Add all other ingredients.

Pour on sufficient olive oil to cover the olives.

Leave for at least 2 days.

Pour back into the jar, and cover.

They will keep for several days in the fridge.

Healthy Lemon Sauce — Mock Hollandaise

Many of us have to watch our cholesterol level, and Hollandaise sauce is one of those embellishments I really miss when serving salmon. I'm happy, therefore, to invite you to share this recipe, which can also be served with asparagus.

Ingredients

2 eggs
2 tbs lemon juice
250ml fish or chicken stock (depending on the dish it is to
    accompany)
1 dsp chopped dill or parsley
salt and pepper, and sugar to taste

Method

Bring stock to boil.

Whisk eggs in a heatproof bowl.

Add lemon juice.

Pour boiling stock onto eggs.

Microwave on very low for 30 minutes, stirring every 10 minutes.

Taste for seasoning and add chopped herbs.

Tip

If you want to cook on an ordinary cooker, put the bowl on top of a pan of simmering water, stirring frequently until the sauce coats the spoon. Do not let it boil.

Crème Fraîche Dressing for Salmon

Here is a quick, foolproof and healthy alternative to the more conventional Hollandaise sauce. What better recommendation for a recipe?

Ingredients

200ml crème fraîche
1 lemon
½ tsp sugar
1 tbs chopped dill
salt and pepper to taste

Method

Grate lemon zest.

Squeeze lemon juice.

Mix all the ingredients together.

Taste and adjust seasoning.

Add chopped dill.

Leave in fridge for at least 30 minutes for flavours to develop.

Index